STRATEGY IN MOTION™

A Proven Playbook for Companies Who Win

DARCY BIEN

HOLON
PUBLISHING

www.Holon.co

ISBN#: 978-1-955342-62-9 (Hardback)
ISBN#: 978-1-955342-63-6 (Paperback)
ISBN#: 978-1-955342-64-3 (eBook)

Published by:

Holon Publishing & Collective Press
A Storytelling Company
www.Holon.co

"I was introduced to Darcy's strategic planning process in 2003. Darcy's facilitation of that first strategic planning session put our company, Stober Drives Inc., on a sustained path of continuous improvement and growth. Most of our major improvement initiatives over the years have come directly through strategic planning, which we repeat every 18-24 months. I attribute our company's positive development and my personal professional development to a great degree to our engagement with Darcy and strategic planning. This book is a go-to guide for CEOs who are ready and willing to do the work."
—*Peter Feil, General Manager at Stober Drives, Inc.*

"Darcy's process brought a high level of structure and accountability to our company's strategic planning experience. She was upfront about how demanding the process could be at times – what she calls the "messy middle." Darcy is a straight shooter with genuine integrity. We had candid conversations and she told us what we needed to hear. These discussions, along with her Strategy in Motion™ toolkit, helped us reach the finish line."
—*Andy Schuster, President at Matandy Steel*

"Darcy has been my much-needed strategic Sherpa! With her help and training, my team and I learned that intentional time on strategy is essential to having an evergreen, successful organization. Darcy not only engages and inspires leaders at a visionary level, she also provides a host of pragmatic strategies that are easy to implement and applicable to organizations of all sizes and types. Leaders committed to their own development around strategy and the success of their organizations cannot skip this essential book about putting your strategy in motion."
—*Ken Elrich, Co-Founder at Solid Blend Technologies, Inc.*

"While developing strategy is essential, so is implementing and expanding it. By golly, Darcy asks tough questions to make sure the strategy is right! The methods Darcy employs have empowered us to achieve excellence. Plus Group has thrived by applying Darcy's strategic principles and translating priorities to actions and results. Darcy provided invaluable input to our processes and has challenged us to not just grow, but to expand by focusing on our purpose and core values as the foundation of all that we do. Darcy's leadership fosters accountability with rigor, intensity and depth."
—*Grant Mitchell, CEO at Plus Group*

"Darcy's Strategy in Motion™ process helped us grow our company, our leaders, and ourselves. She is a great listener and has a knack for sniffing out differentiators our executive leadership team had missed. Darcy's process helped refine our cultural cornerstones – including our purpose, mission, and core values. Her "Listen and Learn" phase with all stakeholders allowed us to create a strategy to move the company forward. Through her stellar guidance, we have capitalized on our strengths and combatted our weaknesses."
—Molly North, CEO at Al. Neyer

"It's a privilege to be in the room while Darcy leads companies through her process. Her ability to implement her Strategy in Motion™ toolkit – while simultaneously helping teams navigate the strategic planning landscape – is like watching a master at their trade. This book provides open access to the exact process Darcy uses to create brilliant strategic plans. She didn't omit any "secret ingredient" as she expertly shares every detail to help strategic leaders stretch to the next level of success. This book will be a tattered guide that never leaves your desk."
—Cyndi Wineinger, Co-Founder & Partner at Stretch Strategic Leaders

"The four years I partnered with Darcy for strategic planning were the most intense intellectual years of my life. Together we facilitated strategic planning programs for more than fifty companies. It was a real joy to work with Darcy and to make substantive differences in our clients' success. Darcy has talked about writing a book for a long time, and I am proud that she has published it. She has always been passionate about making these strategy tools accessible to everyone. I am confident that if you listen to her and trust her system, your company will be on a path to greater success."
—Laura Brunner, President & CEO at
The Port of Greater Cincinnati Development Authority

"Darcy's process is extensive, but complete. Her unique "listen and learn" approach involves all stakeholders and she helped chart a stronger course for our company. She focuses on execution – unlike many strategic plans that sit on a shelf. Darcy's Strategy in Motion™ process helps you scale, not just grow, and I think that's why organizations are successful with her approach."
—Dennis Andersh, CEO & President at Parallax Advance Research

"We have worked with Darcy since 2011. Her process challenged the way we think and the way we view our business and the markets in which we operate. In the first session we had with her in 2011, she unearthed the single largest strategic issue facing our company. This led to a major, multi-year shift in our go-to-market strategy which has paid significant dividends in the form of both revenue and profit growth. Darcy's new *Strategy in Motion*™ playbook is a fantastic amalgamation of all of the tools, approaches, processes, etc. that she has used to guide us over the last 11 years. She shares relevant examples that help readers bridge the gap between principle and practical application. This book will be valuable to both companies new to strategy and those who have been working the process for years. I look forward to having this book as a reference for our strategy team as we look to continue to scale."
—Dan Puthoff, CFO at JBM Packaging

"Darcy helped our young and growing craft brewery become more surgical about who we were going to be and how we would get there. And, more importantly, who and what we were not going to be. She masterfully elevated our day-to-day mindset and guided us to a higher altitude of thinking through a time-tested strategy process. Her process enabled us to prioritize our SWOT, establish core truths about our business, define core values, and develop strategies to hold us accountable. She's done a tremendous job helping us focus to pave the path for growth and expansion."
—Brady Duncan, Co-Founder at Madtree Brewing Company

"When it comes to strategic planning, Darcy Bien's expertise and advice cannot be matched. She's guided hundreds of companies to embrace and achieve their vision of success. It all begins with a commitment to the Strategy in Motion™ process. This book gives you all the tools you need to prepare for business and personal success. On a personal note, as a professional facilitator working with nonprofit organizations, my clients have found Darcy's tools to be not only helpful but necessary when engaging in strategic planning."
—Kathy DeLaura, Managing Director & Owner at Partners in Change

There are many people to thank for getting this book published! My Dad is "why" I wrote the book. My mom is the unsung hero in my life. Family and friends graciously listened, pushed, and stretched me through each phase of development — a seven-year process. Thank you to my team and my clients who share my passion for strategy. It is a tremendous gift to work alongside you each day.

Contents

In Memory of My Father

"Have you published anything yet?"
—Ken Misiak, my Dad

Why I Love Strategy

My Dad, who passed away from cancer in 2013, was an entrepreneur and a visionary. He spent countless hours thinking about and creating new ways to solve the problems that beset a range of industries. I enjoyed hearing the latest "idea" that he wanted to run with — and he had many! He was most excited when diving into the next new business; he loved working for himself, and he would joke, "I've been successfully unemployed for years."

If you run a business, you know ideas are never in short supply, whether it's a new invention, a unique service, or an idea for growing and thriving. The real challenge is taking those ideas and implementing them effectively. This is where many people, like my Dad, struggled; he was a big-picture guy, great at visioning, which allowed him to secure seed money easily, but he never broke through the $1 million mark for any of his businesses.

He was in good company: 96% of businesses are smaller than $1 million,[1] and less than half of startups survive beyond five years. This was my Dad! When action plans and additional resources were needed, things went downhill, and all his great ideas couldn't help him. Implementation and follow-through were not his sweet spot.

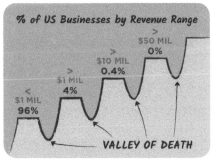

Generating ideas requires a particular way of thinking; building im-

---

1   Harnish, Verne. *Scaling Up*. Gazelles Inc., 2014.

plementation plans and acting on them requires a distinct mindset. It takes planning, a systematic process, investment in the leadership team, and cash to work through the growth phase: this is why strategic planning is critical.

His Favorite Question

Thinking back, I don't know if my career was a reaction to how he approached his business endeavors — maybe. With a Mechanical Engineering degree from Georgia Tech and five years at Procter & Gamble, I thought an MBA from Harvard Business School was the icing on the cake. Along the way, I was able to take my first steps into building strategy, and, more importantly, executing on it. Shortly after my MBA, I joined a strategy-focused consulting firm and committed to helping businesses find the path to growth through effective strategy.

I'd always enjoyed writing and wanted to author a book; I just needed to find a subject that I was passionate about to which I could add value. A master of the "strategic pause," my Dad would wait until he had full attention for his next thought. Every time I spoke with him about my career goals, he would ignore what I was saying, do his famous strategic pause for effect, and then ask, "Have you published anything yet?" He believed publishing books was the ticket to real stardom. When I proudly shared my new accomplishments... I knew it was coming... "Have you published anything yet?"

My Dad, Ken, with Lily

Well, no, Dad, not yet. Until now.

If my Dad had spent more time planning for the future and less time talking about it — or had hired a Sherpa to guide him through each step — I would have a nice trust fund! Today, I am that Sherpa, supporting leaders and their companies through planning their futures and achieving growth. And this book? I wrote it for my Dad, who didn't have a Sherpa but would have been significantly more successful with one!

The Final Farewell

Dad's last visit was for my daughter's first dance recital. Lily told him, "My teacher said we must do our best, smile, and have fun."

She loved to dance, always with a huge smile. During the recital, though, we noticed that she sometimes made the moves only on her right side. No one cared; we loved every minute, although we were curious.

Driving home, we asked her, "Honey, why did you only do one side of the dance?" Without a pause, she replied, "My teacher said the other side was 'optional'." We laughed all the way home.

Lily's teacher knew it didn't matter what these girls did, as long as they did something! Strategic planning is similar; it doesn't matter what you do, as long as you at least do something and decide to plan for the future. It doesn't have to be all or nothing — you get to decide what parts are "optional."

Dad, I did my best, and with this book in my hands, I'm smiling and having fun.

Preface

*"We cannot solve our problems
with the same thinking we used
when we created them."*
—Albert Einstein

Strategy — Why Don't We?

Imagine we're sitting in your office or eyeballing each other on Zoom. I ask you, "How much time are you and your leadership spending on strategy?" Most leaders answer in subdued tones because they know it's not enough:

When I hear...	»	I call this the...
We've been successful so far.	»	"Crossed fingers" strategy
It's too complicated.	»	"I know what I know" strategy
I don't know where to start.	»	"I'm ok for now" strategy
I just need to hire...	»	"Downward spiral" strategy
We don't have time for strategy.	»	"I'm too busy fire-fighting" strategy

My personal favorite

Despite everything written about work/life balance, leaders spend most of their time *in* the business, putting out fires, handling "issues," and trying to get the results they want from employees.

On average, **companies spend <5% of their time on strategy**. This is an extraordinarily small amount of time to develop a long-term vision for their company, understand external trends and challenges, or figure out what they want to accomplish in the next three years. The benchmark we have seen with our clients is leaders of companies who are winning in their industries **invest 20% of their time on strategy**. This includes strategic assessments, reviews, communication, and direct work on goals and priorities.

How do you close the gap between the <5% and the 20%? You need to create "strategic capacity," AKA the time to plan, develop, and execute strategically. Here is the reality — leaders of the company own and are responsible for vision, three- to five-year goals, and creating the roadmap for getting there. This is critical work, and most of the time, it means you need to enable others to take on *running* the business, so you can focus on *leading* it.

Busting the Myths

For every reason business owners give for not committing to team-based strategic planning, I have answers. For example:

We've been successful so far. — Past success does not guarantee future success.
Strategy is too complicated. — It doesn't have to be.
I don't know where to start. — There is help out there!
I need to hire that perfect person. — Structure follows strategy (not the other way around).
We don't have time for strategy. — If not you, then who?

The reality is most of the companies I work with have been successful and have operated with an informal "strategy" — albeit reactive vs proactive. After all, they know (to some extent):

Who they serve *(AKA their market)*
What they offer *(AKA their products and services)*
Where they operate *(AKA their geographical scope)*
How they compete *(AKA their strategic focus:*
differentiation, low cost/
cost leadership, or market niche)

Myth #1: Small businesses *don't* have (or need) a strategy. The reality is most successful small company Presidents do have a plan, although it may not be on paper. They would not have made it past a startup without a plan. Entrepreneurs are normally amazing technicians in the business and have a plan, although they may be the only one who knows it, because it is in their head!

Their plans are based on current assumptions of how they believe things to be. This works, until things change, and their assumptions need to be challenged and potentially updated. Usually, these "informal" plans consist of using what they already know and doing more of the same each new year.

Myth #2: The way we have always done it will always work. This myth is based on the *hope* that if we continue doing the same thing, but harder, it will all turn out ok. The big question, "Is what you're doing getting the results you want?" If so, then keep doing it. If not, stop hoping. We need to remember how fast-paced our world is today and how technology is a game changer. Saying "this is the way we've always done it," can be the slow decline of a business. Don't be caught listening to music on a Walkman!

My clients have made it past the "cash crunch" and are experiencing a revenue plateau. Many grew by successfully serving a market niche, then they added customers, but they just can't break through to the next stage. Fundamentally, they're STUCK; they are running flat or on a decline, with no apparent external condition driving that change. All too often, they're economically dependent on two or three key customers.

They need to think differently, but instead, they try working harder and faster. It doesn't do the trick; they're still stuck. Unfortunately, some avoid the necessary investments (for example, marketing to generate targeted leads so they can say "no" to unprofitable accounts) until the pain becomes so great that they must change; change is painful, especially when forced rather than chosen.

Many leaders are so busy working *in* their business they don't take time to plan. It's a case of both unchallenged assumptions and misplaced priorities.

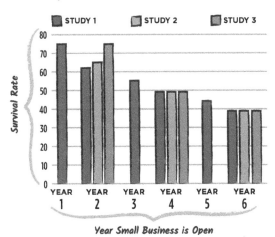

FIGURE P-1
SMALL BUSINESS SURVIVAL RATES

For new companies, survival rates are poor: only 50% make it to five years, less than 40% survive their sixth year — if you've made it past that point, congratulations!

Think back and notice the pattern of spurts of growth then getting stuck again each time — for subtly distinct reasons, but stuck, nonetheless.

The brutal truth is that companies stop growing because as desperation creeps in, they are:

- *Less attractive* to the market
- *Less desirable* to their best employees or incoming management who want to be associated with success
- *Less powerful* with key customers who have more bargaining power and forever want better pricing.

If they have investors, they start looking for a clear path to their exit.

Many of my clients have used a formal team-based strategic planning process to get un-stuck; **you need to lead and manage more to grow successfully and reach the next level.** This requires grit and new ways of thinking. Over and over (and over and over), I remind my clients that strategic processes and tools work — they are best practices and just need to be customized to work best for you.

If you want to be among the top performers, you need to start running your company differently and hiring the people who can help you achieve that growth. Strategic planning is the perfect place to start.

The Pain of Change

Since 2002, I have facilitated strategic planning for hundreds of organizations as a partner with my strategic planning firm, Partners in Change. In 2019, I co-founded Stretch Strategic Leaders to integrate leadership development and training. We started with the Cincinnati Regional Chamber of Commerce — running their *Strategic 8* public strategic planning program. Partnering with Aileron, an organization focused on bringing Professional Management to small businesses, I gained experience and wisdom facilitating strategic planning programs and sessions for their clients. With a track record of facilitating almost 400 plans, I came to understand planning was the easy part — it's the *implementation* that was the real work.

Leaders need a mindset shift to take on strategic planning — it begins with vulnerability and humility. I know you don't have all the answers, and guess what, no one expects you to! Planning is stimulating, needs a team, and takes commitment, rigor, and curiosity.

The real work starts in the execution, where the pain of implementation shows up fast. People generally don't like change; there is comfort in following the path well-trodden if what we are doing is working. We all know change is inevitable: you either proactively manage it, or you are forced into it. Think of competitors, suppliers, or customers who are not around anymore. Why? What happened? They ran out of cash, got stuck, or gave up and sold. It was too hard to change.

I Wrote This Book For...

My goal for this book is for every company to realize the benefits of strategy and what happens if you don't take time to plan. Being around visionaries and passionate people is why I love working with small- to mid-sized growth-oriented businesses. These owners started with an idea and a sense of purpose — they may have needed help putting it down on paper, but they had a reason to go out on their own. Most are outstanding technicians, but many are in the weeds of running their business and limiting their company's potential, which constrains their growth.

Strategic planning helps owners work *on* the business and not *in* it. It includes documenting what is in their heads using a team-based process to gain alignment and commitment to achieve a shared vision.

There are three things to remember:

1. Past success does NOT guarantee future success;
2. "If we want different results, we need to do different things;" and...
3. As Lily reminds us, everything is optional. Start where you can — do what you can do.

IMPORTANT!!!

As you dive in, remember to make the strategy process work for *you* — you'll see results year after year as you get better at it. It's worth your time and investment! I highly recommend outside support like a guide or trained facilitator, especially if you get stuck. The key is to keep moving forward.

In Each Chapter

I will take you through my *Strategy in Motion™ (SIM) Process* in sequence with each phase explained. There will be some background to the concepts that underlie the planning process, and then you can put those into action with your team.

I suggest you use this book as a work in process playbook. Feel free to highlight, circle, write in the margins, and put it to use! Most of all, enjoy learning and have fun! Read the entire book first, take lots of notes, then share it with your team, and, when you're ready, develop your own strategic plan.

www.stretch-sl.com/SIMtools

I will share all the tools you need, which you can download by following the QR code seen here. Make them work for you, and remember, you've got this!

Dan

NOTES

CHAPTER 1

The Why

> *"Running a company without a strategy is reckless."*
> —A.G. Lafley and Roger Martin[1]

Hope is Not a Strategy…

One day, a message popped up on my computer screen with some warning about my printer's ink pads. I hit "ignore" and hoped it would keep working. For three more months, every time I saw the message, I hit "ignore" again and kept hoping, and like magic, the printer kept working. I do strategy for a living, so I knew this would come back to bite me. Unfortunately, every time I went to pick another printer, I was overwhelmed; with so many different models and options to choose from, I'd freeze.

One morning, as I was preparing for a kick-off meeting with a new client, the inevitable happened. The magic failed — the printer broke, and I was in a panic at full throttle. I needed copies — quickly. After two hours of trying to navigate online print services (which is about as intuitive as a Chinese puzzle box), I hightailed it to an office supply store and grabbed a printer (which my husband later told me had horrible reviews), then rushed home to complete my preparation.

As I completed the session with my client, I thought about my printer, and a Japanese proverb came to me:

> *When you're dying of thirst,*
> *it's too late to think about digging a well.*

I was dying of thirst, all right. My pain level was HIGH, and I was consumed with putting out the fire. I noticed how comfortable I got ignoring the pop-up warnings and hoping it would never happen. I was burying my head in the sand about my printer's impending demise.

---

1   Lafley, A.G., and Roger Martin. *Plan to Win: How Strategy Really Works.* Harvard Business Review Press, 2013.

Until pain from putting up with the status quo is greater than the pain of change — we don't act. For a while, "hoping it will keep working" *can* hold things together, but eventually, something will break. We've all been there. Hope is not a strategy.

As a consultant who helps clients with strategic planning, I know firsthand how hard it is to change. It's as though we must be pushed into it; **statistics show proactive change happens less than 10% of the time**. We are creatures of habit, and our brains like to follow familiar pathways — after all, it makes life easier.

Hey! I'm Talking to You

Over a couple of decades, I have facilitated hundreds of strategic plans with clients in different industries and sizes. My goal is to first help business leaders know why they should "take time for strategy" and how to get started.

Two questions for you:

1. **Why would you proactively choose to embrace change?**
   ANSWER: Strategic planning *manages* change by, first, understanding "why" we need to change and, second, to avoid the pain of firefighting. We do this by understanding what assumptions we are using to run our business. Those may have changed and, therefore, we need to change the way we think. When pain is avoided, fewer resources are wasted, decisions are made calmly (not from panic), and the company can be on the same page as to what the strategy is and what the plan is for executing it.

2. **Is the timing right for you to begin strategic planning?**
   ANSWER: It depends. A few things to consider: Is your business day full of fighting tactical fires? Is your team getting the results you want? Is most of the future of the company in your head?

   If yes, then strategic planning would be helpful!

What is Strategic Planning?

Strategic planning has been around forever but the concept was formally defined by the military. The word strategy comes from the Greek στρατηγία (stratēgia) — *the art of generalship.*

Wikipedia defines strategy[2] as a "plan to achieve one or more long-term or overall goals under conditions of uncertainty."

There's nothing more uncertain than being at war — wouldn't it be helpful to know *how* to win battles when you are in a strong position *and* a weak position? A sixth-century Chinese military strategy book, *The Art of War*,[3] written by a general, political adviser, and philosopher, tells you how.

2   "Strategy." *Wikipedia*, Wikimedia Foundation, 15 June 2022, https://en.wikipedia.org/wiki/Strategy
3   Tzu, Sun. *The Art of War*. Filiquarian Publishing, 2007.

So, what does having a plan to win mean in the context of business?[4] Just as in war, we need to win in business, strengthening our position to overcome the competition. How you do that comes from understanding your strengths and weaknesses, those of your competitors, and planning accordingly. Beyond beating the competition and winning new customers, you determine which battles to take on and which to walk away from. In strategy, we want as many wins as we can get with as few wasted resources as possible. Remember, most of my clients are "resource constrained," so managing and allocating the resources is a critical responsibility of leadership. This is as much about saying "no" as it as about saying "yes."

How to Win

Lynda Applegate[5] compares strategy to soccer, using the phrase "look up." Great soccer players don't look at the ball when dribbling; they look up and out — constantly scanning the field, looking at the defense (the competition), and using their team's strategy to win the game.

Strategic planning is very similar; you're creating space and time for your business to look up from internal concerns, looking out at what is happening in the market, and then **creating a plan to win**. You'll make time to be curious about your market, your competition, the economy, changing technologies, and disruptive ideas.

The Purpose of the Strategic Planning Process

My clients run businesses ranging from $10-$200 million in revenue, with 20-500 employees.

When I survey them about their key challenges as leaders, their biggest concern (as seen on Figure 1-1 on page 14) is understanding the critical *external* changes that will impact them, including future economic conditions.

If you are a typical small business owner and spend less than 5% of your time on strategy, it is tough to find time for that research. Your team also has knowledge and ideas, although when are they able to share? As a result, it's difficult for the company to proactively prepare for new trends or challenges.

---

4   Listen to David Kryscynski's video "What is Strategy?" on how to win with strategy: https://www.youtube.com/watch?v=TD7WSLeQtVw
5   Lynda M. Applegate, Baker Foundation Professor at Harvard Business School, also serves as the Chair of the Advisory Committee for Harvard University's Master of Liberal Arts in Extension Studies degrees in finance and management. Lynda also plays a leading role in developing and delivering HBS Executive Education Programs for entrepreneurs and business owners.

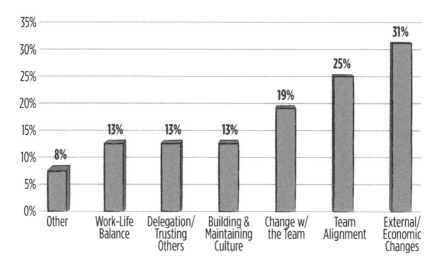

FIGURE 1-1
KEY CHALLENGES FOR BUSINESS LEADERS

Incidentally, team alignment is the second most critical challenge for businesses.

For some of my clients, strategic planning is the first time they have looked "up" and "outside" of their company as a team, had open conversations about it, and created a longer-term plan to act on new opportunities and threats.

The good news is — strategic planning done the right way tackles many challenges companies are experiencing. If your team is made a part of strategic planning, they will feel empowered and take more ownership in keeping the company successful for the long-term.

Strategy Helps You with Team Alignment

A strategy provides focus and helps you choose when to say "yes" and when to say "no" to specific initiatives or actions; a good plan helps you allocate resources to where you should invest in order to win. It also helps you walk away when the investment is not worth the potential return. Having a well-communicated, unified view will result in your employees supporting your choices and understanding why it's a "yes" or a "no."

Figure 1-2 on page 15 shows how when asked about the perceived benefits of strategy, allowing the company to say "no" is the top benefit. Why would that be the case?

Saying "no" doesn't come naturally. Still, when used judiciously, it separates "yes" leaders who may have grown revenue — at the cost of lower profits — from those who said "no" to the poor opportunities, had more managed growth, and, most importantly, generated *better profitability.*

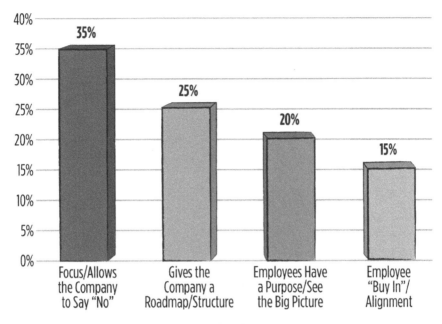

FIGURE 1-2
THE BENEFITS OF STRATEGY

One of my clients had 1,500 customers, yet less than 10% of them contributed 80% of the profit. They had a strategic priority called "Starve the Problems" for two years. They developed an aggressive pricing strategy to discourage unprofitable clients (effectively saying "no") while keeping their profitable clients (saying "yes").

The net result was an increased profit for less work!

So, the bottom line (literally) is saying "no" to unprofitable clients to increase profits — put that in your back pocket for future use.

Strategy and Alignment

I love the way Molly, a long-term client, the President of a design-build company, described the benefits of strategic planning:

"First, having a well-articulated strategy helps all employees have purpose in their work. If carried out properly, employee and company goals align to achieve the strategy. Prior to our company having a well-defined strategy, we had people moving in different directions pursuing opportunities that they, individually, thought were valuable, but could not get support from other functions of the organization. A well-defined and communicated strategy now ensures our people are working on a common plan."

How Do You Know You're Ready?

As we discussed, many businesses plateau at specific revenue markers for their industry — to get off the plateau requires a growth-focused business model: being profitable (so you can invest in opportunities) and having an aligned organizational structure (so rather than wearing multiple hats, leaders are experts in their area).

Laura Brunner[6] created the Evolution of Strategic Planning model, which describes the stages companies go through as they build their strategic capacity. To move through the stages takes commitment and investment. I work with many companies going from Stage 2 to Stage 3, which includes external based research.

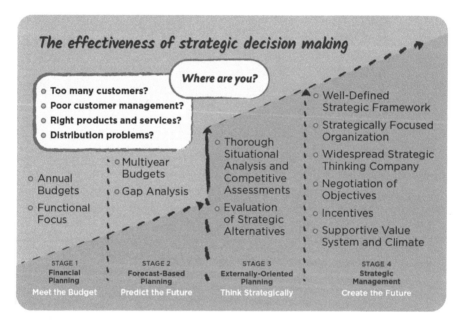

FIGURE 1-3
THE EVOLUTION OF STRATEGIC PLANNING

Stage 1: Meet the Budget. Most of our time is spent looking at revenue and profit in the rearview mirror and short-term planning, usually annually. When a business starts adding metrics, specifically leading indicators (pipeline, lead-time, customer, and employee satisfaction) and investment in the operation is needed to grow, they're ready for Stage 2.

Stage 2: Predict the Future. During Stage 2, a company starts to think three to five years ahead instead of just planning for the upcoming

---

6　Laura Brunner was a Founder Partner of Partners in Change, one of my companies. Now, Laura Brunner is the President and CEO of the Port of Greater Cincinnati. Thank you, Laura, for the mentoring and support!

year. Leadership starts looking for the gaps in infrastructure, especially human talent, which need filling if growth is to be a possibility.

In a Stage 2 business, some critical responsibilities *are still* a part of someone's job. For successful growth, it's essential to hire people who have the competencies and knowledge — for example, someone in Marketing or HR. These are roles that require subject-matter expertise. As an alternative to hiring, a cost-effective way to acquire these capabilities is through outsourced support, like specialty firms, consultants, or fractional C-level people. A key outcome of a strategic planning process is identifying and prioritizing the staffing needs to scale the business for growth.

Stage 3: Think Strategically. Over 30 years ago, when I worked for Procter & Gamble, I found this quote: "Leadership is the art of getting someone to do something you want done — because they want to do it."[7] I think that is also a quote from BBC's *The Office*!

I think about this a lot with strategic planning. Most times, when thinking three years into the future, we know this will require "change" and we can see that what we are doing right now just isn't working. Remember, if you want different results, you have to do different things. Involving key leaders in the strategy is critical to help them know why change is needed.

It's time to switch from playing Chutes and Ladders to chess. Stage 3 companies have a sustainable model, have done some planning, and are ready to take it to the next level. The company leaps from internal considerations to a need for *external* knowledge and understanding. Thinking strategically means looking for market opportunities and threats; it's time to examine competitors, industry research, and customer feedback to make informed decisions about the right chess moves. Because the leadership team has grown from just a few to six or eight key people, it is also critical to align around a longer-term growth plan.

Stage 4: Create the Future. Strategy is now integral to the company's operations; it has grown from the leadership team to energizing and engaging the entire organization. **Having supported the process so many times, it's my favorite moment to watch — when leadership teams *wake up* and become "Alive at Work."**[8] This book cites studies that indicate we are more engaged and happier at work when we are given time to be creative and involved in planning. And of course, it's fun to dream and even better to achieve results. Maybe it's time to start that dream journal.

Companies in Stage 4 have a solid strategic framework and wide-

---

7   O-Toole, James. *Leadership A to Z: A Guide for the Appropriately Ambitious*. Jossey-Bass, Inc, 1999.
8   Cable, Daniel M. *Alive at Work: The Neuroscience of Helping Your People Love What They Do*. Harvard Business Review Press, 2019.

spread strategic thinking; they are fully committed to a strategic planning process, they utilize proven tools, and most importantly, they have a capable strategic planning team driving the process forward.

Time to Stop Being Reckless

 I can't stress this enough!

The leader's primary responsibility is to proactively prepare for the company's future. Here's the reality: **it's your job as a leader to *define* the future. If you don't, who will?** We can all agree that change will happen, and we can either manage it preemptively or wait until we are forced to mutate. It's not so very different from your fifth-grade science class on genes. Mutation will happen in the market, whether you like it or not. Your job is to proactively manage the change and choose a direction.

You'll need a learning mindset and team mindset because the first time you work on real strategy, it may be challenging; I promise that it will get better with practice. As a first-time planner, think of strategic planning as an opportunity to *listen and learn*, *document* what's in your head, and *share* it with others. Then *implement*, *keep learning*, and *continuously improve*.

Why Don't People Want to Change?

Many years ago, I asked my organizational development partner, Cyndi Wineinger,[9] "Why don't people change and adapt to new ideas?"

Her answer was simple: "They don't want to."

When she first said that I was ready to argue... *What about the plan? What about the new reality that will require them to change? What about the...?* But people change only when *they* want to. We're only human, after all. This is a massive opportunity for small companies — you need to figure out *why* your people would wish to change. **Engaging them in strategy is a huge part of a successful change process.**

Involving people beyond top leadership when developing your strategy allows them to contribute ideas to those goals and provide reasoning to support them. When they participate in the process, they need to be involved, understand their role in making things happen, and own the outcome. Employees want to be involved, heard, and trusted. As we know, many plans sit on the shelf because someone not involved in the process had it handed to them but wasn't motivated to act on it. It may be a great plan, but without buy-in, that's all it will be — a great piece of work, gathering dust, with no impetus to make it happen.

---

9 I've known Cyndi since 2018. She's an expert on all things "people" related and she knows how to effect change. **She has spent years studying the effects of change on the brain.**

If companies tell me they have a strategy, I ask to see it, at which point they get uncomfortable. The plan may be a PowerPoint presentation for the board or a past plan that may or may not be relevant. Unfortunately, many times, the plan is in the owner's head, and they tend to tell employees about it *only* on a need-to-know basis. I reference this *Dilbert* a lot. If it's not *visible* and *communicated*, it might as well be "the warranty for your chair."[10]

One of my go-to Dilbert cartoons!

The most significant (and tricky) part of becoming a strategic leader is motivating your people to embrace change with understanding and enthusiasm. This is one of the most rewarding tasks ahead of you.

Strategy in Motion™ — IDMTSU

Across my career, I developed a strategic planning process by curating best practices from all the "strategic gurus:" Michael Porter, Jim Collins, Robert S. Kaplan, and many of my clients. I have a phrase I use a lot with my clients, "I did not make this shi*t up (IDMTSU)..." meaning these tools have been proven to work. I use 80% of the same process with my clients and customize about 20% of the process to meet each of their needs — this is critical. In the remaining chapters, I will walk you through how to use the process for yourself and your company.

Today, **Strategy in Motion**™ is a well-proven process for growing small to mid-size companies. As part of the process, several tools are available to help you gather data and guide you toward your strategic plan.

The Four Phases to Strategy

My **Strategy in Motion**™ **Process** has four phases, or steps.

10   DILBERT © 1999 Scott Adams, Inc. Used By permission of ANDREWS MC-MEEL SYNDICATION. All rights reserved.

Phase 1: Listen and Learn. You start the process by assessing what you already have available and determining what further research is needed. Many call this an **environmental scan**. This includes an *internal* analysis with customer and employee surveys and an *external* analysis, including industry, market, and competitor research. For first phase planners, I encourage my clients to take an active role in the research to really understand the current reality — more on this later. The goal is active listening and learning. This means rolling up your sleeves and doing some of the research. This changes as companies grow and get larger. **My goal is for my clients to first do it themselves before they ask others to do it.** This is a good rule of leadership, by the way!

Phase 2: Plan Development. This includes your core purpose, core values, vision, and critical strategic choices requiring investment and focus. This is an interactive process with working sessions, allowing different perspectives, and then coming together behind an aligned three-year strategic plan and one– to two-year strategic priorities.

Phase 3: Implementation. This is where the rubber meets the road with scorecards, action plans, and communication focused on the strategy. **Many companies get anxious when accountability increases, and some even freeze waiting for perfection, or worse, they "put it on the shelf" because they are afraid to move forward.** Our process and tools will help you over the speed bump. You will need to reduce the need to be perfect and focus on making progress.

Phase 4: Strategic Management. The company starts to link the strategy throughout the organization, allocate resources to support the plan, and continually assess the plan's effect, making necessary improvements. Communicating the strategy becomes a critical responsibility of the leadership team. Cyndi Wineinger, the "people" expert, reminds our leaders, "The vision bucket is always half-empty," which means constant cheerleading (yep, that is what it takes!).

You stick with your plan, you improve, and eventually, it's time to assess how it went and update. As you work the strategic process, you will add tools and build capacity. It is amazing to see how far a company has come in three years of commitment to the process. **Rinse and repeat, not one and done.**

Strategic planning improves with practice!

Chapter Summary

In this chapter you:
- Looked at the cost of ignoring the warning signs, hoping, and doing the same thing year after year. This approach only works for so long — eventually, something will break. Hope is NOT a strategy.
- Understood what strategic planning is and how it helps you win in business. Critically, you have to look up from the day-to-day to gather the information you need from outside your company to create an effective strategy.
- Examined the stages of how companies approach planning, including the incremental results you achieve when you put strategic planning in place as part of your management processes. You established which stage you're in and confirmed the role of leadership in providing the impetus for strategic planning.
- Acknowledged that planning is needed, but execution requires buy-in from your people — all your people. Implementation is the hardest part of the strategy, mainly because people resist change. It's your job to inspire them.
- Grasped the four phases of **Strategy in Motion**™, the foundational process you'll use to take your company on this strategic planning journey. Realized that **IDMTSU** (I did not make this sh*t up) and these really are proven best practices to help companies be more successful for the long-term.

And how's my printer? The best part is that the new one works better than my old one. I'll be proactive next time round, hopefully. ☺

NOTES

CHAPTER 2

Understanding Strategic Planning

"If you don't know where you are going, you may end up some place else."
—Yogi Berra

Two Parts: The Strategy and the Plan

Consider that strategic planning has two parts — "strategic" and "planning:"

1. The "strategic" embraces *what* you want to achieve, or put another way, what it means to win.
2. The "planning" is *how* you will get there and what choices you will make so that you *will* win.

The "what" and the "how" — it sounds like a formula for sorting out any kind of life goals, and indeed it is. I'll show you how I used strategic planning in a life situation in a moment, but there's one thing missing. It's the "who," and I don't mean the 1960s rock band.

Jim Collins had a foundational belief that "good is the enemy of great."[1] Lots of organizations are "good." They have been in business for many years and are doing "good" work. I would submit, just by reading this book, your company is a "good" company. The question is, do you want to be "great?"

For me, strategic planning is choosing to make your company *great* — like winning a race versus participating in the race. This is:

Being proactive versus reactive.
Making choices and trade-offs versus saying yes to everything.
Gaining alignment versus telling people what to do.

Notice that the third item, gaining alignment, requires great leadership. In Jim Collins' words, he'd say, "WHO, *then* WHAT, *then* HOW," where the "who" is **your current and developing *great* leaders.** ← *the "who"*

If you're an owner or leader who wants your company to be great,

---

1   Collins, Jim. *Good to Great*. Harper Collins, 2001.

you need to decide what it will take to make you great. One thing is certain: you can't get too great without strategic planning — figuring out the "what" and the "how" — but to do that, you need great people "on the bus" so to speak. And, as we know, great companies make hard choices so they can win!

Let's Talk About Winning

In my work with many different companies, they've all had a unique definition of winning and wildly different choices for how to win.

It's essential first to understand how the current ownership defines winning. If I questioned the key leaders in your company about what winning would look like, would they have similar answers or have distinct responses?

This may mean they all have a *different* strategy in mind.

Ask Key Stakeholders

When I ask business owners what their vision is or key goals are (what they want to see in their future), they say something along these lines:

I want more time to work "on the company."
I want to take a vacation and not worry or work the entire time.
I want to be financially independent ($2M in investments and $1.5M in a 401K) and provide for my family and employees.
I want to retire (by the time I'm …) and transition to my children.
I want to take care of my employees (secure a future for them).
I want to sell my company (for $20M) and then sit on the beach/create a non-profit/travel the world/write a book/climb Kilimanjaro/retreat to my tropical island paradise.

ok, so this one is mine ↗

Whatever the vision looks like, owners have goals, and their version of winning is to fulfill that vision and accomplish those goals. They hold their personal goals with passion, although unfortunately, many have never shared these goals.

Business owners (including family members, members of the board, or investors) are **key stakeholders**. Their goals matter and the first step of strategic planning is to find out what's important to them. Also important are the goals of **company leaders**, which aren't always aligned with the key stakeholders.

What About Business Leaders?

When I say, "company leaders," I'm talking about the company's executive/senior leadership team or other rising stars. These people are in the day-to-day of business, so I ask them what winning looks like for them. They usually offer a mix, for example:

We need to make profits (15% of top-line revenue).
We need to grow (to $50M).
We need to beat the competition (in 1 out of 3 deals).
We need to expand what we offer (at least one new product or service per year).
We need to expand geographically (to EMEA and South America).
We need to hire great people (to help with all this).

Here is the opportunity: ***we need to align the owners with the company's key leaders.*** The people who are running the company will execute the strategy. This is one of the most important outcomes of a good strategic planning process.

By the way, you don't have to be aiming for double-digit growth to benefit from a strategy! The benefit of strategy is alignment of shared goals of what winning looks like.

What is Winning?

If a "vision" is a long-term outcome and a "goal" is a way of measuring if you're reaching it, what is "winning?" Both business owners and leadership teams often define goals connecting to their personal vision. But that *may not* define what it means to win as a company.

Winning is about setting your sights on something outside yourself, even outside your company. Let me go back to my race analogy.

What does it mean to win a race? In a race, you might want to:

- **Come in 1st**, AKA be a **market leader**.
- **Be fastest in your group**, AKA be the **most innovative in your industry**.
- **Be in the top 10**, AKA the **preferred choice in your local market**.

There are many ways to define "winning," but notice how great winning choices relate to how the company is *perceived in the market* and that those winning choices are *measurable*. How you define winning is critical for your business leaders to lock onto going forward.

> *Jim Collins didn't research large companies because he thought you had to be big to be great. He used big companies because they have lots of DATA, and unlike private companies, it's available. Everything his research tells us is as relevant to small companies as large ones.*

> *And if your goal is three vacations a year, rather than a private island, or an all-day hike every Wednesday rather than climbing Kilimanjaro, that's fine. Now, we need to align your goals to the company and you're a perfect fit for the **Strategy in Motion™ Process**.*

As a client and CEO of a Power Equipment Distributor company said to me, "The brave pick one." There is no better advice I can give you for choosing a vision and a goal — pick one destination. It takes bravery because we always want to hedge our bets — having only one chip on the roulette table sharpens our thinking and keeps us single-minded.

How Are You Going to Get There?

Once you've defined **"what" it means to win (the "strategic" part),** then you will choose **"how" you're going to get there (the "planning" part).** Good strategic planning starts with understanding what the key stakeholders' goals are. This is in the hands of the owner(s) (and potentially some other invested parties). Planning continues with defining what it will take for your company to win. This is the responsibility of your key leaders, and I highly recommend it be done by an expanded leadership team, not just the owner and the key executives. It is critical to engage next level "strategic" leaders so they can understand the "why" and know how they can help.

the "what"
the "how"

The remainder of strategic planning is taking those key stakeholders' goals, building your definition of winning around them, and developing the plan for how to reach those goals.

Darcy Runs a Marathon

Chapter 1 included an overview of the **Strategy in Motion™ Process.** I want to expand on a few key concepts I used while planning to run my first marathon. There was no **SIM** back then, but I've linked my journey to my process.

It's 1999 — I'm studying at Harvard Business School. My fellow students are crazy, goal-oriented people, so no surprise when a bunch of those friends decided to run a marathon. Spurred on by mass frenzy, I create a *vision* to complete my first marathon within a *goal* of less than four hours. My typical run is around six miles, so 26.2 is a stretch. Yes, I have always had a goal-oriented mindset!

I was already a runner, but I needed a training plan, AKA a strategic plan, to not just finish the race but "win" by hitting my stretch goal.

Step 1 of strategic planning is research, feedback, and bench-marking (**SIM Phase 1: Listen and Learn**). I talk to seasoned marathoners and research how to train for a marathon. I choose the Cape Cod event because the timing works, it is close by, it's a beautiful place, and I have never been there. I also realize quickly that I need to start training to increase my mileage.

Then I move to **SIM Phase 2: Plan Development**. This involves assessing my current reality with a very tried-and-tested SWOT analysis.

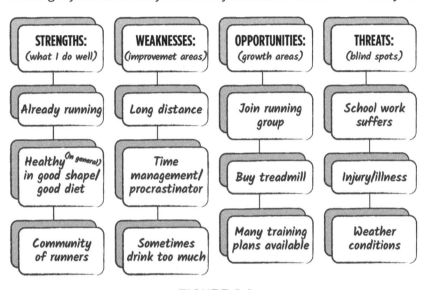

STRENGTHS: (what I do well)	WEAKNESSES: (improvemet areas)	OPPORTUNITIES: (growth areas)	THREATS: (blind spots)
Already running	Long distance	Join running group	School work suffers
Healthy (in general) in good shape/ good diet	Time management/ procrastinator	Buy treadmill	Injury/illness
Community of runners	Sometimes drink too much	Many training plans available	Weather conditions

FIGURE 2-1
SWOT ANALYSIS

As you can imagine, my SWOT isn't the same as for my friends, specifically, my roommate Page, who had already qualified to run the Boston Marathon. My strategic plan is different from Page's because it is customized for me to reach *my* vision and goals. Page runs *a lot faster than I do*, so her training and goals are different.

Once I have my strategic plan in hand, the real work is next — **SIM Phase 3: Implementation**, AKA the training! No one tells me how hard long runs are; they conveniently forget to mention how much time it will take and how horrible it is to run in cold, rainy Boston weather. I adjust my strategic plan multiple times, as my school workload is heavy, and there are other fun things I want to do instead. I also adapt my training plan for each week and measure my weekly increase in miles and time running. Did I mention how many times I fell during long runs? Or the time I was starving, and when I got home, tried to make rice, and forgot to put in the water? **None of it was easy!**

I needed support!

The last step — **SIM Phase 4: Strategic Management** — involves managing the changes and adjustments as an ongoing process, unique to my situation. This includes communication, support, and a continuous assessment of my plan — thinking about each run as part of the process — not single events. I had to give up things I enjoy (like late-night parties). I move forward, improving my miles and times each week. Fortunately, I train alongside friends, and we support each other. Interestingly, we all have different goals and choose different races, which result in unique training (AKA strategic) plans.

We still get together every year!

When the time comes for me to run the Cape Cod Marathon, I am scared out of my mind and feel there's no way I will finish! Luckily, I have the **Party of Five** (see the picture), **my support group** (which I identified in Phase 1 and confirmed in Phase 4) cheering me on at different parts of the race — this is critical! At about mile 14 and another hill, I am dragging. Page jumped in the race and ran a few miles with me! Honestly, this memory still brings tears to my eyes.

It was so difficult AND so amazing. In the end, my time was 3:57 (yep, I beat my stretch goal by three minutes!). Thank goodness for my support group. It took commitment, hard work, and a little pain, but it was totally worth it.

In my marathon example, I only had to convince *myself* to train, but I needed *my friends* to support my choices! The Party of Five, was a huge part of making it through the intensity of Harvard Business School. Page is on the far left, and the crazy part is that 25 years later, we are all still friends, very active in our communities, still running and, most importantly, continue to support each other through all our seasons of life's ups and downs!

For a company to develop a strategy, you need others to help, and you need to gain alignment from them and the company as a whole, on what it means to win and what you want to achieve (i.e., your vision and goals).

All successful strategic processes engage the leadership team, management team, team members, customers, and sometimes the entire community. Gaining support pays enormous dividends when it is time to implement; you have people ready and willing to get on board and go into action — prepared to run a marathon.

If your company is new to strategic planning, the construction of the plan needs a foundation to be in place. These six key strategic concepts underpin your strategy:

1. Our **purpose** — why we exist as a company
2. Our **core values** — how we operate to be successful
3. Our **core focus** — where we win
4. Our **brand promise** — what makes us different
5. Our **vision and stretch goals** — where we are going
6. Our **strategic priorities** — critical areas of focus

The first four are critical to a first-time planner. A lot of time is spent defining these. After that, you revisit and assess how you are "living these out."

For concepts 5 and 6, you're moving into strategic planning. As you saw in my marathon journey, I had to have a vision and a stretch goal to proceed.

Visioning — It Makes Us Happy!

Cookbooks and food magazines have it figured out — they feature gorgeous photos as a vision, leading us to believe we can re-create the dish or dessert just like the picture. We see this picture, and we are excited to give it a try! If it were a text-only recipe, we probably wouldn't be interested — behold the power of visual vision! If my vision is to create a cake that looks just like the

one in the book, and my goal is to have people swoon from the taste, I might not attain either, but I'll have gotten a lot further than I would without the vision and goal.

In the stark reality of the pandemic, the cake that got baked for us in 2020 was not fun for most companies. The worldwide crisis upended expected outcomes; we felt we'd lost control. The main lessons were resilience (we have to keep going), purpose (survival), and

> ultimately vision (where's the best place we can get to right now). 2021 only brought more challenges, but through it all, we occasionally looked up and considered where we wanted to be when this would all be over. We started to believe it would be possible to reach a better place.
>
> Strategic planning is about choosing the path to do the hard work to get to that better place (vision) and then building the plan to reach the goals. Executing on that plan is by far the most challenging part, but **it's the vision that keeps us going**.

It was the vision and goal — and the Party of Five — that kept *me* going. Without those, I would have found it hard to focus on strategic priorities (training) and the necessary changes. As I walk through the nuts and bolts of strategic planning, you'll see how critical each of these items are.

It's a Process

In practice, what is my strategic planning process? Here are some pointers:

- It's a process you perfect with practice. It is not a one and done.
- You work with a team to develop a strategic plan by understanding key stakeholder goals and developing a shared vision. The plan will be assessed and adjusted as you gain more knowledge during implementation.
- You will evaluate and update your plan regularly, monthly, quarterly, annually, and rebuild every three years.
- The tools are proven and will work about 80% for all companies. It is critical to customize to work best for your company.
- It typically takes three to four months to complete the strategic planning the first time around (Phases 1 and 2 of the **SIM Process**); then the real work begins with communication and execution.

Tell them again, and again, and again, and again!

The specific process I will walk you through is the **SIM Roadmap**, which can be seen at the top of page 31. It covers the essentials for each phase — what content I will cover and what tools I will share with you.

That's strategy in a nutshell — it starts with a desire to change, a vision, and a stretch goal (run a Marathon in less than four hours), then developing a strategic plan (training plan to go from running six miles to 26.2 miles). Now, the hard part — it takes discipline and dedication (running, running, and more running), tough choices (exercising and drinking more water rather than wine), and a lot of communication and support (my training buddies). I'm not going to lie, it's a little painful. After all, it takes stretching if you want to go from "good" to "great!" A snake sheds its skin because it needs to grow, but that new skin will be vulnerable and a little uncomfortable. If the snake didn't shed, it would never stretch and grow and might possibly die. Growing pains are good, especially if you want to win!

The critical thing to remember is that you will approach strategy as a *process*, and it gets more "right" every time you do it.

STRATEGY *IN MOTION*

① LISTEN AND LEARN
 » Complete strategic assessment
 » Understand stakeholder goals
 » Listen to employees and customers
 » Analyze external environment

② PLAN DEVELOPMENT
 » Agree on current reality
 » Define desired state
 » Determine strategic choices
 » Outline strategic priorities

③ IMPLEMENTATION
 » Create scorecards and plans
 » Update structure
 » Link to teams
 » Communicate to organization

④ STRATEGIC MANAGEMENT
 » "Look up" monthly
 » Assess quarterly
 » Update annually
 » Invest in training

Chapter Summary

In this chapter, you:
- Examined what strategic planning is, including vision and goals for both owners and leaders.
- Reviewed what winning means for your company and where to focus to define it.
- Learned about the **Strategy in Motion™ Process** in a practical (non-business) example. Remember, strategy is a lot like running a race. You get to decide which race, what it means to win, and the develop the plan to make it happen!
- Appreciated the power of vision and goals to keep you on track.
- Embraced the vital strategic concepts that are the foundation for your strategic planning.

I hope you are already envisioning your own **Strategy in Motion™** as you read this book. Remember, keep taking notes, and the best way to learn is to discuss and tell others!

NOTES

STRATEGY IN MOTION™

PHASE 1: Listen and Learn

CHAPTER 3

Listen and Learn: Data Gathering

"Focus on the Opportunities and starve the Problems."
—Peter Drucker

Stepping into *Strategy in Motion*™

Where is your business today, and what do the business owners and leaders want moving forward? These are the questions you will answer in this chapter.

In an article by Pat Lencioni,[1] he reminds company owners there are certain activities only they can do. One of these is achieving *strategic clarity* with their leadership team, starting with a clear understanding of what goals are essential to the owner(s) of the company.

In This Chapter

PHASE 1 LISTEN AND LEARN

STRATEGIC MANAGEMENT
LISTEN AND LEARN
STRATEGY IN MOTION
IMPLEMENTATION
PLAN DEVELOPMENT

» **Complete** Strategic Assessment

» **Understand** Stakeholder Goals

» **Listen** to Employees, Customers, & Advisors

» **Analyze** the External Environment

---

1 Lencioni, Pat. "How CEOs Should Spend Their Time." March 2018. https://www.tablegroup.com/how-ceos-should-spend-their-time.

In this chapter, we're exploring the goals and dreams of key stakeholders, establishing where we are today, and starting to build a strategic planning team.

The key strategic questions you're trying to answer are:

1. How are we currently doing, and what trajectory do we believe we're on?
2. What is important to me as a key stakeholder?
3. How do I define success?
4. Who should be involved in the process?

Business Owners and Their Goals

It's important to remember each of us have our own definition of success. If you stay true to your definition, you have opened the door for progress.

Business owners are key stakeholders, and strategic planning should start with a clear set of goals that the key stakeholders determine they want from the business.

CASE STUDY

Health Care Communications Distributor

A while back, I had an opportunity to work with a growing distributor of communications devices for the health care industry. The silent owner hires Lou as the General Manager because he "just wants a GM to run it for him."

Lou's excited for the opportunity and sees lots of potential for growth if he can secure necessary investments in infrastructure. He schedules a meeting with the silent owner.

"Hey, I thought I would take the company through some strategic planning," he announces.

The silent owner is... silent. He is unsure what strategic planning is, so Lou jumps in again. "It would be very helpful to know how much you want to grow."

The silent owner quickly responds, "I think I am as tall as I'm going to get."

Lou is astonished, but not really surprised, by the answer — the silent owner is not thinking about the business at all. He doesn't have long-term growth goals. He has been pleased with his business lifestyle up to this point and wants Lou to take care of it for him.

> The story does have a good ending. **Lou bought the company from the silent owner, has committed to strategic planning, and annually shares long-term goals with his team.**

Often, the owner and senior management are not aligned with company goals, and this leads to a lot of frustration and, at times, distrust. **Great companies share common goals.**

Questions in key stakeholders' minds can include things like:

How do I want to spend my days?
Am I interested in growth?
Am I or the business constrained by debt?
What about the children? What are my goals related to the company or their chosen futures?
Am I feeling fulfilled? Have I lost my purpose?

Meanwhile, senior managers might be more focused on:

When can I hire _____ role(s)?
Can we afford to _____ ?
What should my marketing budget be?
Will our new product/service launch on time?
I need a vacation!

A critical part of strategic planning is collecting differing viewpoints around common goals that satisfy the owner(s) *and* can be built upon to create a strategy. To begin with, discussion and adjustment is needed to match stakeholder goals with the strategic plan objectives. This becomes a bit more complicated when there is more than one owner and potentially even more complex when there's family involved.

It is essential to understand what's important to the business owners (both personally and for the business) and ensure *realistic* goals. It's great to have a glorious vision and goals for the future, but if the goals are not realistic, the parties need to redefine and agree on what the reality is and what's achievable in practice.

Owners and leaders need to be on the same page, so I ask owners to share their business and personal goals to start the strategic plan conversation. My first question is:

"Do you, the owner(s), want to grow and invest in the company?"

The owner(s) often do not share a passion for growth with their executives and are happy with a lifestyle business.[2]

A "lifestyle business" is a business set up and run by its founders primarily with the aim of sustaining a particular level of income and no more, or to provide a foundation from which to enjoy a particular lifestyle. The owners/founders are comfortable and are not interested in the changes and challenges of scaling a business.

I have worked with many companies under $10 million who are not about top-line growth. These smaller companies still benefit from strategic planning, but their goals are built around profit, long-term sustainability, and possibly an exit strategy.

Remember that over 96% of companies are less than $10 million and a good proportion of these are lifestyle businesses. Nothing wrong with that, just make sure your leadership team is on the same page. If not, this can cause a lot of missed expectations.

The owner(s) also need to determine:

1. **What is important to me (personally) for the next five years?**
   More time with the family? Prepare a family member to move into the business? (Remember, it's important to ask family members if they share the passion for the business. If not, find out why versus assuming they will change their mind). *Enjoy life more? Work more? Take a real vacation?*

2. **How does this business help me reach my goals?**
   Delegate and build trust so the business can operate with me on the terms I want? Develop an agreement for how owners or family members work in the company? Delegating does not mean you are giving away your own superpower. Think of delegating, as elevating. It develops leaders and frees you up to do what only you can do for your company. Hopefully, you have realized by now, strategy will not be successful without full buy-in by the owners.

3. **To what level am I willing to invest in the company — time, resources, cash?**
   Less time? Willing to invest? Need more resources?

Let's see how **Strategy in Motion**™ helps key stakeholders answer these questions.

---

2 "Lifestyle business." *Wikipedia*, Wikimedia Foundation, 27 December 2021, https://en.wikipedia.org/wiki/Lifestyle_business.

The Phases/Who Does What?

Phase 1: Listen and Learn has four sections. In this chapter will cover the first two:
- **Complete strategic assessment**
- **Understand stakeholder goals**

You'll undertake three activities for these two sections.

The Activities Overview

The two sections will require some independent work and some collaboration. Here's the map for your activities, whether you're a business owner or a C-Level executive, General Manager, or other senior manager tasked with reaching strategic goals.

> **Activity 1: Complete Strategic Assessment**. This task captures what you know today about your business, what work has already been done, and identifies where the gaps are.
>
> **Activity 2: Understand Stakeholder Goals**. What is important to the ownership in the next three to five years? This task captures what the key stakeholders want and are willing to do. It includes collecting important performance indicator metrics and key organizational goals. In addition, complete the **current momentum**. What do the past three years of financial data tell us about the next three years? The combination of stakeholder goals with financial history and projections show gaps. These are compared and debated to ensure the leaders align around the reality.
>
> **Activity 3: Assemble the Strategic Planning Team**. Who are the team members that can carry the strategic planning forward?
>
> **Activity 4: Confirm Your Strategic Process Owner for *Implementation* and *Strategic Management***

Initiated by the business owner(s) or top executive(s). Completed by executive(s) collaborating with owners.

Activity 1: Complete Strategic Assessment

Search and reapply is one of my key learnings from my first real job at Procter & Gamble, an engineering role. When you started any project, you were required to find anyone and anything available to help you before you developed the plan. I learned quickly that this was well-invested time to improve the outcome of every project. If you're embarking on a strategic planning project, it can feel daunting, so let's start with what you *already* know and then uncover everything you *don't* know. The assessment ranges across the whole process of strategic planning and implementation, so there may be *lots of gaps*, and that's to be expected at this stage.

Beginning with an audit allows you to uncover work you have already done that the team might use, reducing the workload and potentially speeding up your efforts, and shortening the planning journey. Additionally, you'll identify items you *don't* have and determine if what you have is still relevant.

The Strategic Planning Assessment Tool

The tool on page 41 (Figure 3-1) is a simple set of statements that need answers: (1) YES (we got this), (2) NO (we need to do this), or (3) DON'T KNOW (not sure what this is or if we have it).

When you tackle this task, slow down and take your time — above all, be honest about where you are. You don't want to build a strategy on a doubtful foundation: it's better to put DON'T KNOW (DK) or NO (N), especially if you can't put your finger on it!

Activity 2: Understand Stakeholder Goals

To assemble key stakeholder (owner) goals, pay attention to three areas — personal, financial, and company. These come from the owners and will include whatever is important for this planning cycle (for example, leadership succession or reducing debt).

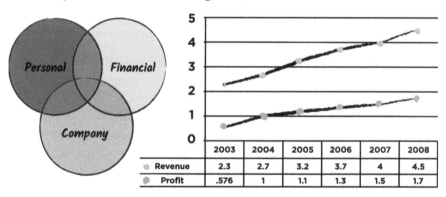

	2003	2004	2005	2006	2007	2008
Revenue	2.3	2.7	3.2	3.7	4	4.5
Profit	.576	1	1.1	1.3	1.5	1.7

FIGURE 3-2
FOCUS FOR STAKEHOLDER GOALS

STRATEGY *IN MOTION*
LISTEN AND LEARN 🔊
STRATEGIC PLANNING PROCESS ASSESSMENT

COMPANY: DATE:	Y	N	D/K
Listen and Learn (Data-Gathering)			
1. We have <u>analyzed our Customers</u> by revenue and profit. We know our Ideal Client.			
2. We have <u>analyzed our Competitors</u> by products and markets and know the top five. We identified their biggest strengths, weaknesses, and threat level.			
3. We have <u>analyzed the Industry</u> and understand the key trends and challenges.			
4. We have <u>surveyed our Customers</u> and know why they buy from us (differentiators).			
5. We have gathered <u>strategic input from our Employees</u> (start, stop, and continue).			
6. We have three years of <u>past financial statements</u> (profit and loss).			
7. We have <u>segmented our products and markets</u> by revenue and profit.			
Strategic Plan (Development)			
8. We have a clear <u>Vision</u> (desired state) in writing and it has been communicated throughout the organization.			
9. We have documented Core Values (operating guidelines) and they are alive in our people systems and all employees know them.			
10. We have a clear <u>Purpose</u> Statement (the why) and our employees are inspired by it.			
11. We have three-year <u>Stakeholder Goals</u>/Objectives (revenue, profit, ROA, sales/employee, others) and the Leadership team understands them.			
12. We have <u>prioritized our SWOT</u> and have plans for the top three in each area.			
13. Our <u>Target Market</u> is clear and our marketing and sales efforts are focused on it.			
14. We know our <u>Strategic Differentiators</u> and measure our Brand Promise (uniqueness / differentiators).			
15. We have made Investment Decisions on each business segment (build, hold, or divest).			
16. We have identified our <u>top Strategic Priorities</u> with champions and measures of success.			

+1 513.807.6647 | DARCY@STRETCH-SL.COM | STRETCH-SL.COM

STRETCH
STRATEGIC LEADERS

PAGE 1 OF 2

FIGURE 3-1
STRATEGIC PLANNING ASSESSMENT TOOL
To download, visit stretch-sl.com/SIMtools or follow the QR code in the Preface

If we were sitting together, here are the questions I would ask you:

What are your personal goals?
What are your financial goals?
What are your business goals?
Are you willing to invest to achieve those goals?
What is your current situation: Financial? Key metrics? Realistic projections based on historical results?
Are your goals aligned with where the business is, what it can provide for you, and what the team would wholeheartedly commit to?
And then, last but not least... **Do you want to invest to grow?**

If you have a family business, a board of directors, or investors, you won't be the sole voice in answering these questions or setting the company's high-level direction. Whether you're 100% the owner or need to work with others, some of your answers will be personal and confidential to you, but you should share as much as you can, as it helps achieve consensus, both with fellow owners and your executive team.

The central decision for the strategy is whether you want to grow or not and, if so, to what ends. It's ok if you don't want to grow, *and* it's still essential to have a strategic plan. Companies that aren't growing tend to decline over time, with the gradual loss of clients and increased lethargy amongst employees. Unless you're planning to wind down (and even then), you need a plan to help you proactively hold your course. Make sure you're clear about what you want and that the other key stakeholders are too.

The Stakeholder Goals Tool

The components of this tool (Figure 3-3 on page 43) help the owner(s) be specific about where they want the company to be in five years and what needs to happen in those five years to achieve those outcomes. Strategic plans are typically for a three-year period — that's the model I use. For the purpose of this task, the key stakeholders want to look out a little further.

The areas listed on the left are generic enough for most companies. I would advise you to answer all of these questions as fully as possible, but you can add additional important ones.

Your BASE year is typically the last complete fiscal year, but if you're in the latter part of the current year, you could choose that. Write the years you are referencing above the columns in the Stakeholder Goals Tool.

As an aside, I've used this tool with more wide-ranging groups of

STRATEGY *IN MOTION*
LISTEN AND LEARN 🔊

STAKEHOLDER /
BOARD GOALS

	BASE	+1	+2	+3	+4	+5
Sales ($M) What revenue goals do you have?						
Profit (Gross or Net Margin (%) What profitability goals do you have?						
ROA (net profit/total assets) What business ratios are critical to you?						
Productivity (Net Sales/Employees) How does productivity need to change?						
What other goals are important to you?						
Culture						
Succession Plan / Leadership Transitions						
Operational						
Personal						

+1 513.807.6647 | DARCY@STRETCH-SL.COM | STRETCH-SL.COM

STRETCH
STRATEGIC LEADERS

FIGURE 3-3
STAKEHOLDER GOALS TOOL
To download, visit stretch-sl.com/SIMtools or follow the QR code in the Preface

key stakeholders, including boards and investors. You can do that too, and you'll need additional meetings to gain alignment. In the end, there should be one aligned list of stakeholder goals with a balance of **financial, personal, and company goals.**

	2021	2022	2023	2024	2025	2026
Sales ($M) What revenue goals do you have?	$53M	$61M	$70M	$75M	$80M	$90M
Profit (Gross or Net Margin (%) What profitability goals do you have?	7.2% Net	7.7% Net	8% Net	8.2% Net	8.5% Net	9% Net
Productivity (Net Sales/Employees) How does productivity need to change?	$245,000 PER FTE	$305,000 PER FTE	5-10% improvement year over year			
What other goals are important to you?	➢ Create Opportunities for employees to grow professionally, ➢ Retention of key employees ➢ Core Values, purpose and shared vision ➢ New Geographic Markets					
Exit Strategy Succession Plan / Leadership Transitions	➢ Add more partners to the ownership group ➢ Improve profit sharing 10% ➢ Consider ESOP in 3 years					
What other Business changes are important?	➢ Increased requirement of minority participation ➢ Protect against economic uncertainty ➢ Provide customers with more options					
Personal	➢ Become a better leader and better communicator ➢ Create a more cohesive team environment ➢ Ensure succession plan is successful					

FIGURE 3-3C
STAKEHOLDER GOALS TOOL — CLIENT EXAMPLE

The Current Momentum Tool

Once you understand the critical stakeholder goals, the next step is to uncover the gaps and constraints to achieve those goals. This is done by: (1) Comparing the stakeholder goals to the past three years of results; and (2) Using the trend of those results to project three years into the future. It is ideal to also share industry benchmarks to help the leadership team understand if you are above or below others. The full scope of the Current Momentum Tool can be seen in Figure 3-4 on page 45.

Although I have heard **many owners say they want to "double the company in five years,"** the reality is that current momentum tells a different story. This tool helps uncover issues and constraints to profitable growth. This exercise allows the leadership team to better understand the past and the change needed for a more ambitious future while making it more likely to happen.

STRATEGY *IN MOTION*
LISTEN AND LEARN 🔊))

CURRENT MOMENTUM ANALYSIS

Column A (actual performance the past three years); Column B (estimate of current year performance); Column C (based on current momentum, forecast the next three years' performance, pending any significant changes).

Measure (define if necessary)	COLUMN A Performance: Last 3 Years			COLUMN B Performance: Current Year	COLUMN C Current Momentum			INDUSTRY BENCHMARK
	20___	20___	20___	20___	20___	20___	20___	20___
REVENUE								
MARGIN								
CASH FLOW								
PRODUCTIVITY (REV/ EMP)								
ADD other Key Performance Indicators:								

FIGURE 3-4
CURRENT MOMENTUM TOOL
To download, visit stretch-sl.com/SIMtools or follow the QR code in the Preface

45

Below is an example of how to use the Current Momentum Tool:

Measure (define if necessary)	COLUMN A Performance: Last 3 Years			COLUMN B Performance: Current Year	COLUMN C Current Momentum			INDUSTRY BENCHMARK
	2010	2020	2021	2022	2023	2024	2025	20____
REVENUE	$10.4M	$12.3M	$14.4M	$16.9M	$18.5M	$19.4M	$20.5M	
MARGIN	42.5%	43.8%	43.2%	41.1%	41%	41%	42%	
CASH FLOW	($59K)	($70K)	$20K	$125K	$50K	$60	$75K	
PRODUCTIVITY (REV/ EMP)	$323K	$363K	$338K	$369K	$390K	$392K	$403K	
ADD other Key Performance Indicators:								
Number of Orders	205	190	341	215	220	230	240	
No Of Employees	39	38	42	49	50	51	52	

FIGURE 3-4C
CURRENT MOMENTUM TOOL — CLIENT EXAMPLE

Note that you can edit/add data rows to this Current Momentum Tool to fit your business. **Remember, these tools need customization for each business.**

Aligning Stakeholder Goals with Current Momentum

As I mentioned earlier, the two prior tasks now need to be set side by side to identify gaps/constraints between stakeholder goals and current momentum projections. As Peter Drucker says, **"Focus on the Opportunities, and starve the Problems."**[3] It's time to work on common goals that, at a high level, bridge the gaps and lead the way to start tackling the constraints while maintaining focus on the opportunities ahead.

The owners' goals are pivotal to this discussion with the leadership team — it may be a tough conversation or not. I've seen both ends of that spectrum and everything in between.

A trained facilitator is a big help. They do this for a living! ☺

Sometimes, owners are unaware of market realities, especially if they're not active in the business or have tended to focus on solving problems rather than operating strategically. None of this is bad — it just doesn't lead to an aligned vision of long-term success.

The point of this part of the strategic planning process is to challenge, ask questions, then gain alignment between key stakehold-

3   Drucker, Peter. *The Effective Executive: The Definitive Guide to Getting the Right Things Done (Commemorative Edition)*. Harper Collins, 2017.

ers and senior management. The final output of the strategic plan is strategic goals, which the strategic planning team must be committed to in order bridge the gap between stakeholder goals and current momentum.

Activity 3: Assemble the Strategic Planning Team

To work through the strategic planning process, you require more resources to gain forward momentum. Just as importantly, the strategic planning process is a forum for discussing new and innovative ideas and considering differing viewpoints, as well as resolving disagreements and coming to a consensus.

In a smaller company, people often wear multiple hats. Even so, it's important to have representation from across the functions of your business, so consider using your trusted advisors or consultants (such as a fractional CFO or CMO) to be part of the team. In larger organizations, the people you're looking for are probably already in-house.

Don't limit yourself to the senior management team — consider including people who are committed to the business, influential within the company, and are "ideas" people. If you see them as key to implementation and/or progressing within the company, this is an excellent opportunity to invest in their capacity for advancement.

Below are the guidelines for picking your strategic planning team:

1. The team is typically six to eight people, sometimes 10 to 12 for larger organizations.
2. One or more key stakeholders, usually owners, will be on the team and provide the team with the stakeholder goals and expectations.
3. Executive/senior management team members should be on the strategic planning team.
4. This process is an excellent opportunity for professional development; you want to make sure you involve key people, especially those taking on more leadership responsibilities or in key roles impacted by the strategy.
5. The initial strategic planning team may or may not be the same team that continues into execution of the strategic plan. The role of the team at this point is to create the strategic plan.
6. **You want the strategic planning team to engage fully in the process and feel like they own the strategic plan.**
7. Ensure all essential functions are represented, including "shared services," if you use that model.

The full scope of the Strategic Planning Team Tool (Figure 3-5) can be seen on page 48.

STRATEGY *IN MOTION*
LISTEN AND LEARN
STRATEGIC PLANNING TEAM

Guidelines to consider:

- Strategic "Planning" team should consist of 6-8 people.
- Members of the Executive team should be on the Strategic Planning Team.
- This may or may not be the same team that continues as the "Strategic Team" or "Leadership Team" moving forward (we may engage people on the planning team who may not be on or remain on Leadership team).
- This process is great opportunity for Professional Development; we want to make sure we involve key people – especially those taking on more leadership responsibilities.
- We want the Strategic Planning teams to fully engage in process and feel like they own their business unit strategic plan.
- Need to make sure all key functions are represented, including "shared services."
- Key Company Stakeholders will provide stakeholder goals and expectations of the team and process.

Potential	KEY FUNCTION REPRESENTED						Key Lead	Has Cap	Strat Thk	Pos Att	Div Tht	Comments
	Pres	Sales	HR	Mkt	Fin	Ops						

Key Lead: Key leader in the organization who will benefit from Professional Development.
Has Cap: Has capacity to dedicate to the strategic planning process and will not be overwhelmed.
Strat Thk: Has ability to be a strategic thinker, has new ideas, thinks big / visionary.
Pos Att: Displays a positive attitude and represents are core values, most of the time ☺ Wants to be included.
Div Tht: Brings a different perspective to the team due to diverse background, experience, length of time. Thinks differently.

+1 513.807.6647 | DARCY@STRETCH-SL.COM | STRETCH-SL.COM

STRETCH
STRATEGIC LEADERS

FIGURE 3-5
STRATEGIC PLANNING TEAM TOOL
To download, visit stretch-sl.com/SIMtools or follow the QR code in the Preface

Who puts the team together? Ideally, this is a discussion between owners, senior managers/board, and the facilitator, if you are using one. Over 20 years ago, when I first started facilitating strategic planning, I assumed it was the senior leadership team. Unfortunately, most strategic plans require more capacity than the senior leaders have, therefore, it is best to engage the next level of leaders in this process.

The President/CEO is the **Strategic Planning Team Leader** and will be accountable to deliver the strategic plan. I have also found it very helpful to also identify a **Strategic Process Owner** to support the President/CEO. This person will be responsible for keeping the planning process moving forward; this may be any of the senior leaders, as long as they have the time, the passion, and are "process" oriented.

Activity 4: Confirm Your Strategic Process Owner for Implementation and Strategic Management

It has been my experience the Strategic Process Owner is a critical role for completing and executing your strategic plan. Many times, the owner/CEO/President is a visionary, but not a process person. I do this with 100% of my engagement and a high percentage of these companies move forward and successfully implement their strategy. It is important — the Strategic Process Owner has the authority to corral executives, strategic and priority teams, and operational teams.

The Strategic Process Owner:

- Manages the process
- Acts as a sounding board
- Helps teams avoid errors — conceptual or process-oriented
- Ensures everything is covered
- Keeps teams on schedule and meetings moving
- Manages personalities, so conflict is constructive
- Ensures a realistic understanding of resources
- Challenges the teams

This is a leader with a passion for strategy!

In a smaller company, this might be a new responsibility for a strategic leader. This is typically a full-time job for a senior project manager in a large company. Fortunately, a few of my medium-sized clients have seen the value of this and have a full-time role, Chief Strategy Officer, which is typically seen only in large companies.

Your Strategic Process Owner should ensure communication, training and development plans are created for the strategic priority teams and anyone else involved in implementation. This is key for roll-out and alignment building.

The training for the strategic process owner is covered in my ***Strategy in Motion*™ *Bootcamp***[4] and offers a deeper dive into strategic planning concepts and available tools. See also Appendix 2.

Chapter Summary

In this chapter, you:
- Examined the importance of the stakeholder goals in driving the company's goals.
- Understood that individual stakeholders often have widely different personal, financial, and company goals that must be aired and reconciled. There should be one aligned version shared with the strategic planning team.
- Embraced the roles and tasks needed to examine the company's current and anticipated momentum and balance them against stakeholder goals.
- Reviewed the available tools to support the first two steps of the ***Strategy in Motion*™** process.
- Appreciated the importance of collaboration and transparency so that the gaps between owner expectation and reality can be identified, setting the scene for finding solutions during strategic planning.
- Envisioned your go-forward strategic planning team and Strategic Process Owner.

---

[4] For more information about Bootcamp Training or for the entire ***Strategy in Motion*™** process, visit https://stretch-bootcamp-training.teachable.com/p/stretch-strategic-bootcamp.

NOTES

NOTES

CHAPTER 4

Listen and Learn: Collecting Feedback

"Feedback is gift! We can't change what we don't know."
—Darcy Bien

Understanding the Reality of Your Business

One of my core values, "Feedback is a gift," has become a mantra. All processes are better with feedback, and strategy is no exception. As many of you know, one of the biggest challenges is keeping the plan from "sitting on the shelf" after rollout. Many companies have baggage because "the last time we invested time in strategic planning, nothing happened." Collecting feedback expands the understanding of what needs to change and engages a broader group of people. This helps keep the plan *moving forward*.

Unfortunately, too many leadership teams plan a full-day working session to discuss strategy without much feedback from key stakeholders (employees, customers, board, and partners). Mainly because they are unsure of "how" to do it effectively and efficiently. Sometimes, they are anxious about "what" will be said, and instead move forward without listening. Leaders often make wrong assumptions because they avoid

collecting and *really looking* at the data. The result is a lack of understanding, buy-in, and engagement from the people who matter most to your business — your employees and customers.

Vulnerability is key to the strategic planning process. If leaders think they have all the answers, the organization limits itself. "Level

5 Leaders"[1] are masters of vulnerability — they gather people around them who ask tough questions and challenge the status quo.

In This Chapter

PHASE 1 LISTEN AND LEARN

» **Complete** Strategic Assessment

» **Understand** Stakeholder Goals

» **Listen** to Employees, Customers, & Advisors

» **Analyze** the External Environment

In this chapter, we're reaching out to hear how others see the company and find out about our markets and competitors.

During the second part of ***Listen and Learn***, you will better understand your competitive advantages (**S**trengths), disadvantages (**W**eaknesses), key ways to grow and improve your business (**O**pportunities), and what may get in the way (**T**hreats). This will be the foundation for the **SWOT**, an alignment tool to understand your **current reality**.

Here are five questions to consider:

1. **What does not fit? Are there activities/products/services we are doing that we should not be?**
2. **What would an outsider do?** Be a "consultant" for a day, and look from the outside in:
   - What would YOU see?
   - What would YOU recommend?
   - What blind spots would become visible to YOU?
3. **Is my organization consistent with my strategy?** If your vision says you want to be a leader, are you investing in market research? Are you the first to try things? Does your resource management support your strategy?
4. **Are our processes up-to-date, or are they "the way we've al-**

---

1 Collins, Jim. *Good to Great*. Harper Collins, 2001.

ways done them?" Remember the definition of insanity — doing this same thing over and over and expecting different results.

5. **What might the long-term consequences of not challenging the status quo be?** Being in denial is a powerful force, so look for decisions you avoid, but you know you need to make.

Experience has shown there is a lot you know and a lot you do not. We all recognize change is inevitable: customers' needs will change, competitors will evolve, and employees will want different things. Embrace feedback and challenge the way you have always done things.

In this chapter, you're preparing to plan. For now, **Listen and Learn** to develop your current reality — where you are now. In Chapter 5, you will start work on **Plan Development** and determine your *where you are now and where you want to go.*

The critical component is to ensure you'll avoid building your strategy on a set of outdated assumptions everyone takes for granted. Some assumptions could stay the same, and many will have to change — but how do you figure out which ones?

I have seen leadership teams metaphorically use The Magic 8 Ball, which, although a fun toy, is not the best "tool" to make decisions for your company's future! An effective strategic planning process challenges how we currently think using upfront research, data gathering, and lots of discussion. That's why I called **Strategy in Motion™ Phase 1** the **Listen and Learn** phase.

CASE STUDY

Packing Company Takes Steps Toward New Reality

I had the pleasure of working with a very strategic CEO, John, of a $350 million packaging company. One of his key stakeholder goals was to grow the company to over $1 billion. Yes, I definitely thought about Austin Powers at the time!

The reality was that the company consisted of mainly "small" acquisitions in three primary business units. John knew he needed a formal strategic process to bring them together. He was willing to invest the time in each business unit. Fundamental industry shifts were happening:

ONE **BILLION** DOLLARS

1. The packaging industry was

shifting away from plastic.

2. Retail was moving to more online sales.
3. Culture was becoming more critical.

John had heard about my comprehensive approach, had a capable leadership team in place, and was ready for the work. His team took to **Listen and Learn** by collecting the data, analyzing it, and conducting direct customer interviews. Then they challenged all their deeply-held assumptions. Fortunately, he had the best Marketing Director, David. David took on the role of Strategic Process Owner. He was critical to customizing the process and tools for each business unit. Fortunately, the business unit leaders were all experts in the field, ready to learn, and most importantly, hungry to plan.

One of John's key business units supplied bags for the retail market. Online buying and e-commerce were just starting to take off and represented a small percentage of retail sales. Everyone agreed that, over time, e-commerce would significantly impact the business — an example of a critical assumption that was shifting. Retail was changing, and the more the team understood why and how, the better they would be at sustainability and adjusting to continue to serve their market.

Another assumption that was changing was how they served the casino market. In the past, most of the packaging was to secure money and coins from the slot machines. As casinos moved to credit and loyalty cards, their need to package coins and notes declined. It was critical to find other "assets" to secure in similar markets.

When we developed the key assumptions at the end of the process, John constantly asked, **"Is our plan designed to live in our 'new' reality?"** Not everything was changing, but it was critical to agree on which assumptions needed to be updated and communicated.

For John, the hard work involved in strategic planning was to research, predict, and communicate the changes in the *current* reality so the company would survive the *new* reality and thrive!

Looking Internally and Externally

Listening and analyzing your findings adds to your understanding of the position of your business with customers, against your competitors, and in the market. You will also uncover what your employees believe needs to change. It's a rich trove of information.

Who Does Our Tribe Think We Are?

One of the purposes of surveying employees and advisors is to find out how aligned they are with the company's purpose, values, vision, and goals, while gathering their perspective on service, customers, and the overall environment the company operates. **If you are a new company to strategy, this is the opportunity to gather feedback to define your purpose, values, and vision!**

Looking internally for information currently buried within your organization and giving everyone a voice in the process is your starting point. You'll use both detailed and short surveys to gain feedback and get to the nuggets of gold.

The External Environment

*And your *theory* of how your business works*

Strategic planning is the perfect way to challenge your current business theories. As we started coming out of the 2020/21 pandemic, business models had been challenged, many things had shifted, and there were so many changes that it felt overwhelming.

I saw increased interest from companies wanting to think strategically, trying to get to grips with an ever-shifting situation. The key is to focus on trends and challenges that will question your business model assumptions. There are no wrong answers because we haven't asked the questions yet! Look for what would impact your company in the next three years, avoiding shiny objects and keeping your attention on your business and the environment you want to operate. There are many opportunities ahead; you just have to be open to consider them.

In 1994, Peter Drucker wrote an article called "Theory of Business." The jewel at the heart of this article is how to recognize when industries and markets are shifting because of a macro trend in the external environment. Honestly, reading this is like taking a sleeping pill. Let me illustrate with a company you'll recognize. *But remember, I love this stuff!*

The Netflix Story

CASE STUDY

There is no way Blockbuster could not have seen the shift happening in their industry. Not everyone wanted to go out in the cold to the store, and everyone hated the late fees. Thinking back, it was like a traditional public lending library with larger penalties!

Meanwhile, in 1997, inspired by Amazon's eCommerce model, Netflix jumped into the space and allowed consumers to choose a movie online and mailed the DVD to them. You sent it back in a return envelope when you were done with it. By 2003, they'd implemented subscription service, personalized their service to your interests, gone public, and shot past one million subscribers.

Looking at where Netflix is today,[2] it's one of the major streaming services for "free" viewing of TV programs and movies, spans over 190 countries with coming up for 200M subscribers, and is an award-winning movie and program creator (36 Oscar nominations in 2021). Competition is fierce, but recognizing that their "stickiness" is *new content that no one else has* ensures loyalty, whatever other services may provide.

What did Netflix do so right (and do they still?)

1. They understood what customers wanted.
2. They used up-and-coming technology.
3. They watched the competition fiercely.

Despite the ever-increasing competition, they worked out how to deliver what customers want and stay ahead of the competition.

Even so, in 2022, for the first time in more than 10 years, Netflix lost 200,000 subscribers during the first quarter. The competition for the "first-mover" is taking its toll. Unlike those who lost the battle, Netflix continues to operate strategically. Let's see how long they last!

Examples of well-known companies who "should have" seen it coming include Service Merchandise, K-Mart, Sears, Toys "R" Us — and the list goes on....

The Competition

Another part of the external analysis is competitor research. Agreeing on your main competitors and/or those to benchmark takes discussion — the more you say "yes" to every opportunity, the more customers you have, spread across too many markets. This often results in a longer list of competitors as a first-phase planner.

I recommend focusing on your primary markets/products/services representing a good proportion of your revenue (say 80%) and maybe six to eight competitors — one for each person on the strategic planning team to research. **Remember, I believe your strategic planning team should roll up their sleeves and do the research. It may make sense for others to support the research as well.** This depends on

2   McFadden, Christopher. "The Fascinating History of Netflix." *Interesting Engineering*, 4 June 2020, https://interestingengineering.com/the-fascinating-history-of-netflix.

your phase of strategic planning and the business needs. Key questions to consider: *What do you know about them? Do you have pockets of information but not a clear overall picture?* Remember, as the saying goes, it's wise to "keep your friends close and your enemies closer."[3] There is so much to learn from your competitors. Look for the Competitor Analysis Tool later in this chapter.

Challenge Your Assumptions

Challenging your assumptions is a critical part of a strategy — don't "trust your gut,"[4] it may not be the best business barometer.

Consider instead trends and challenges that could highly impact your success or might lead to the failure of your company. These will help you understand market shifts, growth rates, economic conditions, and technology changes. Take time to "look up" and understand the changes happening in your industry and with your key competitors. Define the external environment for the next two to three years: understand what is changing and why.

If you've been working *in* your business, this is what working *on* your business looks like.

The Role of Research

As markets fluctuate, trends change, and new competitors emerge, research becomes critical for growing your organization. It provides the foundation for prioritizing and maximizing your resources and getting to the heart of what customers want. The company needs to adapt to market trends and client needs — what is essential to change to keep pace?

Valuable information should be shared with the team and across the organization; this is the time to get everything on paper and, more importantly, discuss the implications. Big businesses have the budget to hire outside firms, but smaller organizations can do their own research to answer questions like:

How do your customers see you?
How do you measure up against your competition?
What differentiates you? How do you measure this?
Why do your best clients choose you? What else would they buy from them?
Why did your prospects choose a competitor?

---

3   *The Godfather.* Directed by Francis Ford Coppola, performances by Al Pacino, Marlon Brando, Paramount Pictures, 1972.
4   Bonabeau, Eric. "Don't Trust Your Gut." *Harvard Business Review*, May 2003, https://hbr.org/2003/05/dont-trust-your-gut

Define Your Research Goals

The scope of the market research will depend on your goals and objectives. For example, your organization may be contemplating a shift in market strategy, but stakeholders aren't yet convinced that it's a smart move. Research can help validate the proposed strategy shift and build consensus.

I love this question on strategic surveys

Research can also help you explore new possibilities. What additional products or services do your clients wish you had? If they could change one thing about your business, what would it be? Research can even uncover your true competitive advantage. It's easy for a "wish list" to grow into an unwieldy (and costly) endeavor, so it's essential to set clear objectives upfront and rein things in if the scope gets out of hand.

What Type of Research Do You Need?

Several types of research can be performed in-house, depending on what will best contribute to your strategy:

- **Customer Research**: Learn how satisfied your clients are with your products/services. Discover what your customers and prospects need and how you can deliver it.
- **Competitive Research**: Research your competitor profiles, pricing, and what they do well or poorly. How many are operating in your area? What makes them successful? What types of marketing are they using?
- **Industry Research**: Trends, threats, major players, growth rates, sales data, social demographic shifts, technology advances, and regulatory changes.
- **Products, Services, and Market Research**: Do your products/services meet the needs of the markets you serve? Which are your strongest markets, and which should you stay in, leave, or begin to penetrate?

There are many other research areas you may dig into as you pursue your strategic planning, but the four above will give you a good starting point.

The Phases/Who Does What?

Let's discuss the final two sections of *Phase 1: Listen and Learn*:
- **Listen to employees and customers**
- **Analyze external environment**

These two steps will require some work by your newly formed strategic planning team to gather the information that will become the basis of your **Plan Development** work coming in Chapter 5.

The key strategic questions you're trying to answer are:

What do we do better than others? What are our competitive advantages?
What is holding us back? What are our competitive dis-advantages?
Why do our customers buy from us? What do they value?
What are other ideas that would support our growth? What else can we do for them?

The Activities Overview

Here's the map for the team's activity for the final two sections of **Listen and Learn**:

Internal Analysis:

Activity 1: Listen to Feedback and Understand the Internal View of Your Company. Use a strategic survey task to capture their perception of your current business and tell you where your strengths and gaps might be. Consider three key groups:

- **Strategic Planning Team**: Deeper dive with the core team to understand places of alignment and strategic issues.
- **Key Leaders/Organization/Board**: Understand how people in your organization and your advisors view the company
- **Key Customers**: Customer Interviews to uncover what customers feel about your company and what they need and want.

Two Parts of the External Analysis:

Activity 2: Explore the Key Competition in Your Key Market. Use competitor analysis to find out how you stack up against your competition, where they're successful and where they aren't, and learn from what they're doing.

Activity 3: Understand Key Macro/Market Trends and Challenges. Use the 7 Factor External Analysis Tool to analyze the external environment.

Initiated by the Strategic Process Owner. Completed by the strategic planning team, other employees as necessary, and strategic advisors (who may not be on the strategic planning team). You will also need to interview a sampling of your customers.

Activity 1: Listen to Feedback and Understand the Internal View of Your Company

As I mentioned earlier, you want to begin with your internal assessment. I recommend (1) Starting with a detailed survey to your strategic planning team, followed by (2) A shorter survey to selected (or even all) employees. These should be customized with your current strategic information, but overall, I use these same questions with about 90% of my clients. If you have the information, then we are assessing how well people know them and believe they are accurate.

Internal Survey Tools

On the next two pages (63 and 64), there are snapshots of internal strategic surveys: the Strategic Survey Tool (Figure 4-1) and the Board/Advisor Survey Tool (Figure 4-2).

The Strategic Survey Tool provides rich information across a range of incisive questions. The Board/Advisor Survey Tool gives your employees and board a chance to share their thoughts and ideas.

Make sure you set a deadline for when surveys are due. As you start seeing the responses, you'll probably find surprises, good and bad. You will want to allow time to summarize the results and share and discuss them in a strategic planning team working session. In my experience, those events can be lively, but the primary goal is to *listen* to what people are saying and take their feedback seriously. Don't think of feedback as criticism, but rather as — you guessed it — a gift.

NOTE: The Strategic Survey Tool can also be shared with trusted advisors, partners, and others who know your business well if you want to spread the net wider.

The Key Customer Interview Tool

You'll want to speak to customers who represent your largest market share, are most profitable for your business, and, ideally, consider your product/service of high value. These are your raving fans and will take the time to talk with you. On page 65 you will find the Key Customer Interview Tool (Figure 4-3).

STRATEGY *IN MOTION*
LISTEN AND LEARN 🔊 STRATEGIC SURVEY

Name (and Role):

1. **WHAT ARE THE CRITICAL CHANGES IN YOUR INDUSTRY/MARKET?**
   Please list **key trends and challenges** in your industry to be considered in the next 2-3 years.

2. **WHAT ARE THE ORGANIZATION'S PRIMARY STRENGTHS (ADVANTAGES)?**
   Consider the competitive advantages you have in the industry/market.
   Strengths. Current capabilities that make you **superior** *to your competition and will help you meet the most important needs of your customers. Ideally these are* **measurable** *differences.*

3. **WHAT ARE THE ORGANIZATION'S PRIMARY WEAKNESSES (DIS-ADVANTAGES / IMPROVEMENTS)?**
   Consider the competitive disadvantages you have in the industry/market.
   Weaknesses: Areas in your **current capabilities that prohibit you from meeting your customers top ranked needs** *or from gaining a competitive advantage. Weaknesses need to be fixed quickly to prevent irretrievable losses.*

4. **PLEASE LIST THE TOP 3 MOST PROMISING AND POTENTIALLY PROFITABLE OPPORTUNITIES (GROWTH AREAS)** to actively and aggressively pursue for Organization. Consider the external environment and taking advantage of trends and challenges in our industry/markets.
   These should focus on ways to grow and/or help the organization become more cost effective.
   Opportunities: Trends, events and ideas that you may capitalize on **to increase results and enhance your business**. *Opportunities may be either internal or external, such as, new technology, cost reductions, greater geographic coverage, etc.*

5. **PLEASE LIST THE TOP 3 MOST DANGEROUS AND POTENTIALLY DEVASTATING THREATS (BLIND SPOTS)** facing Organization. Consider the external environment and focus on threats over which you have a degree of control.
   Threats: Possible events **outside of your control** *that you need to plan for or decide how to mitigate.*

6. **WHAT IS THE PURPOSE OF THE ORGANIZATION?** Beyond making a profit… what is the ultimate reason (The Why?) you are in business?

7. **WHAT ARE THE ORGANIZATION'S CORE VALUES?** What are the essential characteristics that define successful team members?

8. **WHAT IS YOUR ORGANIZATION'S VISION?** Where do you see Organization in 5 to 10 years?

9. **WHAT ARE THE MAJOR STRATEGIC ISSUES?** What are the key questions to address?

10. **WHAT IS THE MOST IMPORTANT FOCUS AREA FOR NEXT YEAR?**

11. **PLEASE SHARE BARRIES TO SUCCESSFUL IMPLEMENTATION OF A STRATEGIC PLAN?**

12. **PLEASE ADD ANY OTHER COMMENTS AS INPUT** into the strategic planning process.

+1 513.807.6647 | DARCY@STRETCH-SL.COM | STRETCH-SL.COM

STRETCH
STRATEGIC LEADERS

FIGURE 4-1
STRATEGIC SURVEY TOOL
To download, visit stretch-sl.com/SIMtools or follow the QR code in the Preface

STRATEGY *IN MOTION*
LISTEN AND LEARN

BOARD / ADVISOR SURVEY

NAME:

DATE:

1. What are the Organization's primary strengths? Consider what makes the organization unique and gives them a competitive advantage.

   _____

2. What are the Organization's primary weaknesses? Consider what is holding the organization back and the competitive disadvantages they have in their industry/markets.

   _____
   _____

3. Please list the most promising and potentially profitable opportunities for the organization to actively and aggressively pursue.

   _____
   _____

4. Please list the most dangerous and potentially devastating threats facing the Organization.

   _____
   _____

5. Where do you see the Organization in 5 to 10 years?

   _____

6. What are the major strategic issues (key questions) which need to be addressed?

   _____

7. What is the most important focus area for next year?

   _____

8. Please add any other comments as input into the strategic planning process.

   _____

+1 513.807.6647 | DARCY@STRETCH-SL.COM | STRETCH-SL.COM

FIGURE 4-2
BOARD/ADVISOR SURVEY TOOL
To download, visit stretch-sl.com/SIMtools or follow the QR code in the Preface

KEY CUSTOMER INTERVIEW

Script: Thank you for participating in this interview. Your insights will play an important role as TBD evaluates its business now and in the future. Below are the questions that will be covered during an in-person or virtual meeting. You do not need to prepare any answers; we are providing this in advance so you have ample time to think about the topics we'll be covering. Thank you for your time, your feedback is a GIFT 😊

1. Where do you see your business in 3 to 5 years? What are your biggest concerns/threats?

2. Why have your chosen to work with ABC Organization? Please help us understand what makes ABC Org stand out or unique capabilities we have?

3. What does a successful partnership with our organization look like? What are your measures of success?

4. Are they other products or services we should offer?

5. What is your current satisfaction with ABC Org on a scale of 1 to 100? If you rated us below, 90%, would you mind sharing why?

6. What could ABC Org do better? Are there things they are doing that they should stop doing or areas or improvement compared to our competition?

7. What is your preferred communication method?

8. How likely is it that you would recommend ABC Org to a friend or colleague? 1-10

+1 513.807.6647 | DARCY@STRETCH-SL.COM | STRETCH-SL.COM

STRETCH
STRATEGIC LEADERS

FIGURE 4-3
KEY CUSTOMER INTERVIEW TOOL
To download, visit stretch-sl.com/SIMtools or follow the QR code in the Preface

Select eight to 10 of your customers and do an in-person, Zoom, or phone interview with them. Send them the questions in advance, although they do not need to prepare anything — you'll be walking them through it. If possible, record the sessions, or if not, have a scribe with you on the call to take notes so that you can focus on the customer. Above all, ask the questions and *listen*. Nothing more. Do not comment on the client's answers or rebut comments you don't like. The latter are the most valuable of all!

To whom should you talk? It depends. For some customers, you might get great feedback from the CEO; for others, it's better to speak to the decision-maker who selected you (not always the CEO), or the primary contact who best knows you and the value you're providing.

This is another part of the research where it is valuable to have more than the sales team participate in these interviews. The more leaders who hear directly from your customer, the more awareness your organization will have. I encourage my clients to spread the load across the strategic planning team. One consideration is that the customer wants to feel like you value their input, so make sure it's key leader to key leader. It's worth the 20 minutes to find out what your customer wants to tell you.

Activity 2: Explore Key Competition in Your Market

Activity 3 is the first part of external analysis — *benchmarking* your key competitors: what their products and services are, how they go to market, what their pricing is, and better understanding their competitive advantages.

The Competitive Analysis Tool

There are burning questions you should have about your competitors. *Who is winning/losing? Who is most/least focused? Who is our biggest threat? How can we defend ourselves? Who may be an acquisition target? What can we learn from them?*

Although you might wish your competition would disappear in a puff of smoke, competition is necessary and healthy — it's beneficial for the customers, for the choice and quality of products and services, and it's good for the market.

Just beware of employee cynicism! **It's critical to know how to win in your markets, and this starts with understanding your competitors.**

In the example on page 67 (Figure 4-4C), a commercial HVAC company did a deep dive into their competitor positioning and marketing to understand how they could improve in those areas.

NAME OF COMPETITOR >>>	ABC - EXAMPLE
Ownership *(who owns)*	Mary Day, President since 2009 Privately owned. On their website, it states they were founded in 2002.
Locations *(local, regional, national)*	Mason, Ohio
Target Market/Customer *(scope of markets served)*	**Specialties:** Industrial Automation, Manufacturing Equipment, Weld Cells, Control Systems, and Electrical Panel Build
Marketplace Position *(What are they known for? What is their tag line?)*	**On homepage:** Let us turn your vision into Manufacturing and Automation Reality! **Also, on homepage (as written):** We Expertise In Wide Variety Of Manufacturing Services From Concept To Installation
% Market Share *(high, medium, low)*	Medium for Industrial clients
Products/Services *(Scope of products/services)*	Industrial Automation, Robotic Systems, Machine Building, Traceability Systems, Panel Build
Purpose, Values, Mission Statement *(What do they have on website?)*	**Our Goal:** Provide our customers with exceptional engineering services and support. **Our Focus is Success**: There is no "one size fits all" solution to your controls challenges.. Our customers have come to rely on us to be their trusted automation provider.
Significant recent events *(lost/gained big customer, leadership transitions, new products/services)*	August 2010: Sold to a new owner December, 2015: Key hires and introduced new product line January 2017: Significant growth July 2018: New location and larger site
Marketing/Advertising *(How do they develop leads and build their brand – social media, key channels)*	**LinkedIn:** 515 followers (last post was 6 months ago) **Twitter:** N/A **Facebook**: New and growing **Instagram:** N/A **Google Reviews**: 20

FIGURE 4-4C
COMPETITIVE ANALYSIS TOOL — CLIENT EXAMPLE
To download, visit stretch-sl.com/SIMtools
or follow the QR code in the Preface

As with your customers, limit the competitors you research to your best markets. Doing six to eight thoroughly is about as much as you can manage, especially if you're a first timer with strategic planning.

I recommend you rely on three primary sources to do research:

1. **Their Website**: Top competitors are not fearful of telling their stories. If they have the advantage, they'll shout it loud and clear.
2. **Your Employees, Partners, and Vendors**: Think sales-people or customer account managers. These folks deal with your competition all the time.
3. **Public Sources**: Think local news, webinars, newsletters, special offers, catalogs, and brochures. Some "mystery shopper" tactics can be helpful here too.

Give your team the list of competitors to divide and conquer with the competitive analysis task. At the very least, you'll have all your information in one place. At best, you'll learn something significant about how the competition operates.

For a first-time planner, visioning is the *responsibility* of key leaders, although it is critical to engage others in the process.

Activity 3: Understand Key Macro/Market Trends and Challenges

There are many tools for analyzing what's happening in the industry market. A best practice is the **PEST** (**P**olitical/Regulatory, **E**conomic, **S**ocio/Demographic, **T**echnological) as well as a few others from Michael Porter's 5 Forces — the result is the 7 Factor External Analysis Tool.

Using this tool, you're looking for macro trends, but sometimes you have to dig deep to uncover what those trends are.

In the completed example on page 69 (Figure 4-5C), the client did a thorough job of understanding trends in each area, figuring out what would play in their favor and what might hurt them, and crafting their response which became part of their strategic plan. Much of this feedback is gathered in the strategic surveys as well.

You can use industry reports, current articles, academic research, commentaries from economists, viewpoints from customers, and much more. Don't skimp — you want to know the trends (otherwise, you're flying blind) but keep it high-level (so you don't get bogged down in detail).

Summarize your findings on the worksheet and condense them to the factors that will either support or challenge your business. I recommend keeping this to one page, as shown in Figure 4-5C.

External Assessment: Looking at the Research

It's time to pull all that data together and prepare for the working session with your strategic planning team. Use the tools to summarize what you found or where there are multiple feedback documents, and analyze that data quantitatively (by the numbers) and qualitatively (by the written comments.) A summary will be much easier for the team to digest and make sure they have the source material to hand. Value the people who love to dig into the data! As a side note, I share all the data and summary in advance so the team has plenty of time to digest the information.

Remember to stay open to all the feedback, especially the ones that challenge your assumptions. These are keys to your future success. Embrace them. They are the unexpected gifts!

	TREND / CHALLENGE	+HELP -HURT	RESPONSE
Markets/Customers/Products How are the markets, customer needs/wants, and products changing?	Increase of customers and markets due to additional drivers (workforce, quality, capacity). The EV market will eventually have a significant impact on the automotive portion of our business. Customers need employees. They cannot get them. Therefore, ROBOTS can really help.	+ +/- +	Adapt our messaging to speak to the pain of workforce shortage while providing the education and solutions to help them adapt to an automation mindset, culture, and cost structure.
Socio-demographic What are changes in demographic, psychographic, and social behavior that may impact your industry and customer?	Not as many people seeking out careers in Engineering / Younger workforce less interested in manufacturing. Workforce life skills, experiences, and motivators are/have changed. Changing priorities and expectations, political tribalism, less general satisfaction with life.	- -	Keep in contact with local high schools, career centers, and community colleges for young talent. Review and identify what the next generation motivators. A positive company culture is always attractive to good employees.
Competition How is the competitive landscape changing, more/less/new competitors, substitutes products/services?	Many opportunities in this field so we should expect competition to increase. Competitors prices will increase sharply, making them easier to compete against. We do need to proceed with caution though, so as not to lose money.	+/- +	Continue to find the niche markets that our company can efficiently excel at. Expand to new technology when it adds value to our core business focus. Monitor competitors
Political/Government/Legislative What are significant changes to regulations that may impact your industry?	Global trend toward nationalism. Continued polarization instead of unity as a nation.	+ -	Nationalism will want products built in America. For America to compete low labor countries, it must automate the manufacturing process. We are in a prime position to help.
Economy What are changes to economic indicators that may impact your industry?	Inflation will increase costs, but also allow for higher prices Low interest rates / good time to borrow.	+	We need to monitor and pass on these costs to our client.
Factors of Production What are changes to key "inputs" – i.e., qualified personnel, raw materials, capital – used to produce your products/services?	Rising costs: shipping and fuel Lack of parts and labor supply chain issues. Delivery dates are absurd. Our supply chain is in shambles.	- - -	Added costs inputs will eventually reduce the CAPEX spending. Continue to search for other revenue streams (i.e. service and support, Product, etc.)
Technology What are changes to key products/ services, manufacturing process, technology, and information systems to stay competitive?	"Green" push may make some technologies obsolete (e.g., automotive exhaust systems) and develop others.	+/-	Technology is constantly being invented, improved, and then implemented and adopted.

FIGURE 4-5C
7 FACTOR EXTERNAL ANALYSIS TOOL — CLIENT EXAMPLE
To download, visit stretch-sl.com/SIMtools
or follow the QR code in the Preface

Out of the Mouths of Babes...

I love the quote on the next page (page 70) from Albert Einstein, and it often makes me think of my youngest son, Liam (see the picture of him at the age of three!).

He looks just like Einstein himself!

"We cant' solve problems by using the same kind of thinking we used when we created them."

Liam has always questioned everything — and still does. From the time he could talk, he wanted to know why things worked the way they worked.

In the third grade, his wonderful teacher, Ms. Smith, challenged her students to create a new company. Liam knew without hesitation what he wanted to do. "Mom, I want to fix problems!"

"Ok, honey," I said. "What is the name of your company?"

I waited with bated breath, and then (seriously, I am not making this up) he said, "Mom, the name of my company will be, **Problems, *No Problem.***"

As I have mentioned earlier, this is a key aspect of strategic planning. Strategic planning is solving for key issues or constraints. This takes a problem-solving mindset, so you don't get stuck in the messy middle. Make sure you have thinkers, like Liam, on your strategic planning team and in your company!

Challenging Assumptions

Sometimes, when a strategic planning team reviews the feedback and research, members will go into denial. This is a sure sign that a deeply held assumption is being challenged. They often rebut with "evidence" from an individual customer or what they heard about a competitor that demonstrates the research is wrong. Tread carefully. You need an open environment for discussion where it is safe to disagree and challenge views. This is when external facilitators are very helpful! As you wrap up the review, note which areas need continued debate. Do you need to unseat out-of-date or downright inaccurate assumptions? Achieving that is a significant victory and is one of the main goals of the ***Listen and Learn Phase***.

Chapter Summary

In this chapter, you:
- Learned the importance of feedback when venturing into strategic planning.
- Considered tough questions to challenge the status quo.
- Understood the research topics that are relevant to the development of a strategy.
- Looked internally for data and information from owners through to employees across a wide range of topics, including the company's strengths, weaknesses, competitors, value to customers, brand promise, and more.
- Researched externally to uncover your organization's market trends, competitor data, and customer perspectives.
- Summarized your findings and conducted a data-sharing meeting with your strategic planning team.
- Identified assumptions that are no longer serving your business.

NOTES

STRATEGY IN MOTION™

PHASE 2: Strategic Management

CHAPTER 5

Plan Development: Current Reality

"An organization's ability to learn, and translate that learning into action rapidly, is the ultimate competitive advantage."
—Jack Welch

It's Time to Develop the Plan

Success! You've completed **Listen and Learn** and gathered data internally and externally. You've even challenged assumptions.

A quick word on plan timelines. My **Strategy in Motion™ Process** assumes:

- Your outlook for your big goals is five years.
- Your strategic plan covers the next three years.
- Your implementation plan covers 12-18 months.

It's time to move forward to the fun part: **Plan Development**.

In This Chapter

PHASE 2 PLAN DEVELOPMENT

» **Agree** on Current Reality

» **Define** Desired State

» **Determine** Strategic Choices

» **Outline** Strategic Priorities

In the next three chapters, we'll complete your strategic plan, which has four sections:

1. Agree on **current reality**. *Where we are now.*
2. Define **desired state**. *Where we want to go.*
3. Determine **strategic choices**. *How to close the gap.*
4. Outline **strategic priorities**. *Focus areas to move forward.*

This chapter will focus on #1 — Agree on **current reality**.

The key strategic questions you're trying to answer are:

What are the key trends/challenges that impact us?
What are our strengths, weaknesses, opportunities, and threats?
What theories (AKA assumptions) need to change?

The current reality provides a bridge from the research, which amassed the information you need to analyze and make decisions, to the foundation of a strategic plan.

What Needs to Change?

I can't say it often enough!

I've seen companies become complacent over time regarding the best way to run their company for the future; the past few years have taught us those norms and assumptions are helpful, but these "theories" need challenging over time. The way we have always done it, doesn't work forever.

When your business started, you created everything from the ground up, made key assumptions about the needs and wants of the market, the scope of your products/services, the best way to operationalize, and many more hypotheses. In the "busyness" of growing a business, shortcuts are a great help, but when I see the same assumptions being used year after year without question, it's time to check and make sure these tenets still hold. You started that process in Chapter 4 — or at least discussed it! In my Procter & Gamble days, instead of "Standard Operating Procedures," we used the term "Current Best Approach" or "CBAs." As you may know, P&G was committed to total quality and had many philosophies. This helped make sure we standardized and continued to improve.

Strategic planning is a great time to challenge your current business theories. During ***Listen and Learn***, did any of the activities make you nervous, paranoid, or downright uncomfortable? If so, you might have already identified your outdated assumptions.

You're looking for five or six assumptions you know you already lean on without question. If you already have them — fantastic! You're going to test those as you create your current reality — they're somewhere in all the data you collected.

Here are some example assumptions to consider from my clients:

- *We have never really needed to invest in marketing, but we are struggling with growth. I wonder if we are stuck and need to think differently about marketing?*
- *Our people are not staying as long as they used to. I wonder if we need to do more formal training and development plans?*
- *Labor is a concern. I wonder if our employee pay and benefits package is competitive enough?*
- *My sales team is focused on price way too much. I wonder if we really understand the value we are providing to our customers, how to measure it, and how to communicate it?*

If yours are similar to these, you're on the right track! Keep challenging!

The Phases/Who Does What?

This step does exactly what it says — defines the **current reality**. You'll be in analysis mode, working through your data, and moving to alignment on where you are now, where the market is going/what relevant factors will influence it, and how you compare to your competition. As a team, you'll come to an agreement on what reality looks like in terms of the opportunities and threats you're facing.

In *Phase 2: Plan Development*, I will cover the first step — **agree on current reality**. You will:

- Use a SWOT tool.
- Start to draft our strategic plan by filling out the first section.

You'll be adding to the plan with each chapter you complete.

The Activities Overview

The early part of *Plan Development* is rooted in analysis and critical thinking: this is a collaborative effort by the strategic planning team.

Here's the map for the team's activity for this first section of *Plan Development*:

- **Activity 1: Determine Assumptions, Goals, and Gaps**. Review your internal and external data and form conclusions from that data. Challenge your assumptions, what goals does the data suggest, what gaps might you have?
- **Activity 2: SWOT It**. Use the SWOT Analysis Tool to create a summarized snapshot of your current reality and answer these questions: *Where are you doing well? Where do you need to make changes? What opportunities should you grasp? What could stand in the way of your progress?*
- **Activity 3: Complete the Strategic Summary**. Complete the

working draft of the strategic summary, which includes your three-year reality assumptions and your SWOT.

Initiated by the Strategic Process Owner. Completed by the strategic planning team.

Activity 1: Determine Assumptions, Goals, and Gaps

Reconnect with your summary from **Listen and Learn**. Look for assumptions that might be outdated, the aspirations that you, your employees, and customers have, the market changes (some of them out of your control as per the 7 Factor External Analysis Tool), and where you are winning and where the competition is beating you:

1. **Survey Data Summary**: From all your survey data, in which areas do you shine, and which require attention? These will contribute to your strengths and weaknesses sections as you complete the SWOT.
2. **The Competition**: What do you notice as you review the competitor data you've gathered? Is there an overall pattern of opportunity or threat? Is it by market, product/service, geography, or client size? Where do you compete most successfully? Finally, what are competitors doing that you should start doing, and what should you stop doing?
3. **7 Factor External Analysis Tool**: What responses did you note as you reviewed the "Trend/Challenges" column? What areas will help your business, and which might hurt it? "Helps" (+) will turn into opportunities, and "hurts" (-) will show up as threats. Complete the columns for +HELP/-HURT and RESPONSE.

Start to think about where you should focus:

- Market segments (industries)? Are you known for strength in specific verticals? Are there ones you should pull out of? Or ones you should break into?
- Products/services? Should you thin out? Double down?
- Geographies? Are there areas where you should pull back? Or ones that you should expand?

Activity 2: SWOT It

Why do a SWOT? Well, it brings together a single aligned version of the **current reality (where we are now)**. This forms the foundation for your strategic plan. I use it as a checks and balances for the strategy. Are we exploiting and measuring our strengths? Are we improving our weaknesses? Are we taking advantages and allocating resources toward key opportunities to grow our business? And, most importantly, are we again protecting any blind spots that could bite us?

It also aligns with your research:

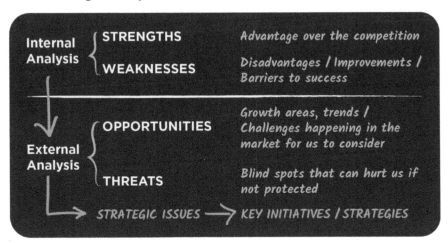

FIGURE 5-1
SWOT BREAK DOWN

The SWOT uses your internal and external analysis to summarize your strengths, weakness, opportunities and threats. As an example, for your strengths, consider feedback from both your employees and customers, then see how they stand up to the competition. During the process, our clients start to have "Aha!" moments. They begin to identify the most critical **strategic issues**, which will drive their key initiatives.

Now that you've mulled over all your summaries (and probably some of the source data), you're ready to complete your own SWOT Remember, you're capturing where you are today, factually. Don't try and fix things in the SWOT — let the ideas that drop out of the SWOT start to gel. We will review, update, and prioritize the SWOT a few times in this process. Remember, this process gets better with practice!

On page 80, you will find an example SWOT (Figure 5-1C).

In a SWOT, it's typical to have around five factors in each quadrant, sometimes more. You're looking for high-level and specific activities the team will be able to explain to others. I have seen some companies tell me "people" are a strength. To which I say, "Every company has 'people.' What is it about your people that is a strength? Be specific so we can exploit it!" Every item needs to be unambiguous. Start with strengths and weaknesses (the internal analysis) and then move on to opportunities and threats (the external analysis).

If you're starting to list more than five items in any quadrant, you'll want to prioritize what you will tackle this planning cycle.

Criteria Examples	STRENGTHS	OPPORTUNITIES	Criteria Examples
• Where are you making money? • What are you doing well? • Business advantages • Core competencies • Advantages of value proposition • Innovative aspects • Price, value, quality	• Long term relationships with customers/vendors (trust factor) • Flexibility in production schedule/ quick lead times • Quality product with low rejections/ clean packaging appearance • Our people- experience with suppliers and customer connections • Easy to do business with, keep customers informed and quick response time • Updated website and videos, strong presence on social media	• New Equipment	Automation, Expand Capabilities (offer new materials) • Hiring new sales rep (be more aggressive) • Training of employees / LMS systems • Production incentives / team based • Freight – are there ways for us to be proactive in this area? Adding another truck that expands beyond our radius • Add platform for customer feedback, suggestions and ideas via surveys from customers and vendors.	• What are the Beneficial trends to grow revenue? • Missing niches • New technologies • New customer needs • Market developments • Business / product development
Criteria Examples	WEAKNESSES	THREATS	Criteria Examples
• What are you doing poorly? • Where are you losing money? • What needs improvement? • Areas being avoided • Resources lacking • Disadvantages of proposition	• Current product line is limited • We are lagging in technology within our production system and machine • Having a difficult time finding quality people and placement, lack of focus on recruiting, training, and education. Lack of retaining and advancement • Departmental communication is lacking – no formal systems • Decision making is long and delayed with a lack of lack of accountability • Currently overpromising - Quoting orders and delivery • Lack of visiting customers and them coming to us	• Workforce concerns - Retention of current core team; retirement of skill sets and key positions; succession planning / bench strength; impact on morale of tenured employees. • Health and Safety training needs increased • Aging equipment and the ability to maintain upkeep • Dependency on key Customers • Concerns on Supply Chain issues - Availability of supply and at what price • Freight – Costs increasing, availability of trucks/drivers and any other logistical bottlenecks • Economic uncertainty – government mandates (vaccine), etc. • Technology – the challenge to stay up to date but not exposed to cyber threats	• What are your blind spots or obstacles to overcome? • Aggressive competitors • Successful competitors • Negative economic conditions • Government regulation • Changing business climate • Vulnerabilities • Environmental effects

(Vertical labels: CURRENT/INTERNAL, FUTURE/EXTERNAL)

FIGURE 5-1C
SWOT: INTERNAL/EXTERNAL ANALYSIS TOOL — CLIENT EXAMPLE
To download, visit stretch-sl.com/SIMtools
or follow the QR code in the Preface

Let's look at the four quadrants step by step. Below is a SWOT Guide to help you:

Strengths (Internal Analysis)

What advantages does your company have? Competitive advantages — better, unique, measurable:

What do you do well? The high value or performance points

What do people in your market see as your strengths?

What factors mean you get the sale?

Can be tangible — loyal customers, efficient distribution

Can be intangible — good leadership, customer intelligence

What unique or lower cost resources do you have access to?

» *Utilizes surveys of employees and customers; understand competition*

Weaknesses (Internal Analysis)

What disadvantages does your company have? Competitive disadvantages — not on par with the competition:

What can your organization improve?

What do you not do well that may inhibit success?

Competitive disadvantages

Prevent you from doing what you really need to do

Weaknesses are internal — within your control

May include unskilled workforce, slow distribution, outdated technology, etc.

» *Utilize surveys of employees and customers; understand competition*

Opportunities (External Analysis)

Circumstances (Industry and market trends/challenges) that may be exploited:

Promising and potentially profitable areas for growth and higher performance

Timing may be important for capitalizing on opportunities

Actively and aggressively pursue

Consider the external environment and ways to grow and improve your organization

Marketplace, unhappy customers with competitors...

May be helpful to use decision matrix to help prioritize

» *Take advantage of trends and challenges in the industry*

Threats (External Analysis)

Circumstances that may inhibit ability to compete, potential blind spots:

What is your competition doing that you should be concerned about?

Most dangerous and potentially devastating area facing your organization

Consider the external environment and focus on threats over which you have a degree of control

Technology, competitor changes, shifts in consumer behaviors, substitutes products

May be useful to classify or assign probabilities to threats

The more accurate you are in identifying threats, the better position you are in for dealing with changes

» *Activities needed to protect against*

The strategic planning team should agree on the SWOT themes and prioritize before proceeding to the next step.

Activity 3: Complete the Strategic Plan Summary

With the SWOT complete and agreed upon, you have most of the current reality work done. If you think of the SWOT in the Strategic Plan Summary: Current Reality Tool (the lower grid in Figure 5-2 on page 83) as a snapshot of today, the three- to five-year reality assumptions (at the top of the section) are your projection into the future. What are the new assumptions you will want to build your business on? Pick three or five years as your timeframe and use your SWOT to list the internal and external assumptions that will drive your business going forward.

There is a different client example for the reality assumptions section on page 84 (Figure 5-2C). On this example, notice that this is high-level, as it should be for a longer-term focus. Detail will show up later in the process.

You want to reach a consensus on every aspect of current reality. Don't put up with divided opinions or competing realities. This stage is *"agree* on current reality" — that is where you want to be before you proceed — in alignment.

STRATEGIC PLAN
SUMMARY–
WORKING DRAFT

CURRENT REALITY
(Environmental Scan - our plan is designed to live in this reality)

3-5-year Reality Assumptions	External (what are the key factors that will impact your organization)	Internal (what will be true internally about the organization)

Competitor Analysis	Competitor	Strengths (Competitive Advantage)	Weaknesses (Competitive Disadvantage)	Threat Level (To-do)

What is our Current State (where are we today)?

SWOT Analysis - Internal	Strengths (Competitive Advantage) What do you do better than others? 1.	Weaknesses (Competitive Disadvantage / Improvements) What is holding your back? 1.
SWOT Analysis – External	Opportunities (Growth Areas) What key "external" activities would significantly grow or improve the company? 1.	Threats (Blind Spots) What key "external" areas to protect against because they may blindside the company? 1.

+1 513.807.6647 | DARCY@STRETCH-SL.COM | STRETCH-SL.COM

STRETCH
STRATEGIC LEADERS

FIGURE 5-2
STRATEGIC PLAN SUMMARY: CURRENT REALITY TOOL
To download, visit stretch-sl.com/SIMtools or follow the QR code in the Preface

3-5-year Reality Assumptions	External (what are the key factors that will impact your organization)	Internal (what will be true internally about the organization)
	Labor constraint – hard to hire people (esp. in construction) and hard to keep people. Lots of people leaving jobs (The Great Resignation) Competition is driving up labor costs. We will continue to invest in our employees and focus on retention strategies	Take on more logistics with key investments
		Continue our strong relationships with customers and implement CRM system
	Customer expectations constantly changing - Deliveries – faster lead times, Jit delivery, customer portal	We will stay with our key distributors and focus on strong relationships
		Stay a family-owned company
	Market/Supply-chain volatility will continue and we need to stay connected	Continued relationship with key sourcing partners
	Technology and automation – this support increasing productivity and use of data	Will keep our current location – will need to expand as we grow
	Virtual – covid has taught "everyone" that you can be productive at home. This may mean less commercial construction with more working from home). Increased demand for opportunities to offer some flexibility to our staff.	
	Larger competitors consolidating the industry– this means bigger centralized offices are making decisions that could have major ramifications for our customer base. Less and less contractors buying direct	
	Inflation – impact on private funding on projects (more put projects put on hold). Our internal costs are going up.	

FIGURE 5-2C
**STRATEGIC PLAN SUMMARY: CURRENT REALITY TOOL
— REALITY ASSUMPTIONS — CLIENT EXAMPLE**
*To download, visit stretch-sl.com/SIMtools
or follow the QR code in the Preface*

Chapter Summary

In this chapter, you:
- Appreciated the role research plays in providing a foundation for your current reality.
- Analyzed what your research is telling you.
- Completed your SWOT analysis to obtain a balanced view of the opportunities and challenges you're facing.
- Finalized your current reality by adding your three- or five-year assumptions, both external and internal.
- Prioritized your SWOT to reach consensus on your current reality.

NOTES

NOTES

CHAPTER 6

Plan Development: Desired State

"It's not my Vision. It's our Vision."
—Andy, President of US Steel Processing Plant

The Power of Core Values, Purpose, and Vision

A strategy without meaning is — well — meaningless. Unless the strategic plan is founded on a meaningful purpose and an inspiring vision backed by core values, it will not have the impact it should. If you think this is the "fluffy stuff," I can tell you employees want to work in a company living its core values, working toward a better future, and sharing a grander "why" than just making a profit. The lessons of integrating values, purpose, and vision with resilience are the core of why I'm so passionate about strategic planning. This is the difference between "good" and "great."

Vision plays a central role in two books that have influenced me the most: *The Road Less Traveled* and *Man's Search for Meaning*.

In *The Road Less Traveled*,[1] Scott Peck reminds us that we all have baggage, and the "road less traveled" is the one where you choose not to let your baggage impact your life… that is resilience! **I often think about the book's opening sentence, "Life is difficult."** The road less traveled is the complex and sometimes painful process of change and positive choices.

Psychologist Viktor Frankl[2] chronicles his suffering as a prisoner in Auschwitz, Dachau, and other camps. He writes, "The prisoner who had lost faith in the future — his future — was doomed." It's a bleak book, but I took away that

---

1   Peck, Scott M. *The Road Less Traveled*. Touchstone, 2003.
2   Frankl, Viktor. *Man's Search for Meaning, Gift Edition*. Beacon Press, 2006.

those prisoners who "had something left to do" had a purpose for their lives and held on more tightly to faith and hope.

You may also be familiar with the bricklayer parable when rebuilding St Paul's Cathedral. When asked what they were doing, one bricklayer described his work as "feeding his family," another was "building a wall." The third and most productive bricklayer said he was "in service to a higher power and creating a cathedral."

The main lessons in both are the integration of resilience, purpose (real meaning), and vision (imagining a better place). Strategic planning is about choosing to do the hard work to get to that better place.

The reality for some companies may not be rosy (e.g., your biggest market is going away, you lost your largest customer, or you are constantly firefighting versus proactive planning). Many times, our current situations seem out of our control. Maybe it's time to get rid of the arsonists! Here is the good news — you have the power to change it.

In This Chapter

"Problems, No Problem!"

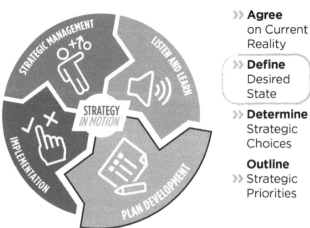

>> **Agree** on Current Reality

>> **Define** Desired State

>> **Determine** Strategic Choices

>> **Outline** Strategic Priorities

We're working on the second section of ***Phase 2: Plan Development,*** which is "define desired state."

You're going to establish who you say you are today and look up and out into the future to create the direction you'll take for the next three years, working toward a longer-term vision five to 10 years from now.

The key strategic questions you're trying to answer are:

Why do we exist as a business? (Purpose)
What critical behaviors support success? (Core values)
Where are we going? (Vision)
How do we define our three-year strategic goals?

Developing these strategy elements takes time, and patience is critical. It will take about one to two years to finalize these, and you will want to involve the organization. That's ok — take the time to communicate and iterate until you feel they represent your company, and your organization is inspired by them.

Having worked with hundreds of companies on these, here are some tips I have learned along the way:

- **Core values** should describe what "successful behavior" looks like at your company. It should be reflective of the founders and key leaders. Be careful if current leaders are NOT living these — this is not ok and needs tackling before the rest of the organization will believe in them.
- Some of the best **purpose** statements came directly from the customers and employees — this is why **"Feedback is a gift."** Asking them why they work with you is a great place start. Also, hearing the history of the company and understanding why the original founder went out on their own can be very insightful to the purpose conversation. Your core values and purpose are foundational to your culture and can last a long time, even longer than your vision.
- And **vision**? "A vision statement says what the organization wishes to be at some future time... in a clear, *memorable* way." To reach memorable requires an effort over time, so be prepared to work and rework it. Your vision typically contains a five-to-ten-year BHAG — Big Hairy Audacious Goal. I am a firm believer in the power of measurable and repeatable visions.

My favorite vision example is "We Choose to Go to the Moon" — immediately you know who said that. John F. Kennedy had a vision on May 25, 1961, of "landing a man on the moon by the end of the decade and returning him safely to Earth." The vision statement inspires others to understand what mankind was attempting to accomplish.

As you can tell, working on core values, purpose, and vision requires time and repeated interactions. I remind my clients not to "put it on a

T-shirt" for the first year or two. Once done, you must commit to living and communicating these. Many companies use visuals and wall graphics. I am a big fan of a one-page strategic infographic for the organization to understand key parts of the strategic plan.

Here's my strategic infographic from years ago:

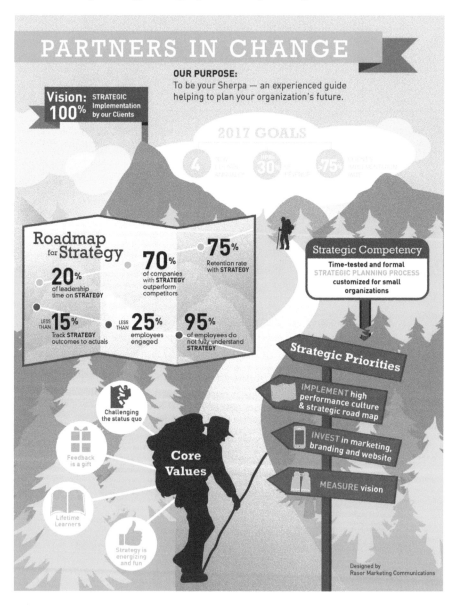

FIGURE 6-1
STRATEGY INFOGRAPHIC (PARTNERS IN CHANGE)

In case it's hard to see, here is the information broken down:

- **My Purpose:** "To be a Sherpa — an experienced guide helping you plan your organization's future." By the way, our clients told us this! Also, remember my Dad and "why" I do what I do — he needed a Sherpa!
- **My Vision:** (AKA the desired state) is "100% Implementation," which ensures my clients don't "get stuck" and move forward to do what they say they are going to do. I stick with them because planning is the easy part. It's the implementation that's hard. This is also an industry challenge I am helping to solve.
- **My Core Values:** Most importantly, I believe strategy is a process and should be fun and energizing (see my core values, AKA critical behaviors). This approach views strategic planning as a learning process (another one of my core values), challenging the status quo (another core value), and remembering you need lots of support.

Defining your culture with core values, a clear purpose, and a vision has always been a differentiator for successful companies. After troublesome years at the start of the 2020s, with labor constraints and economic pressure, doing this work became a requirement for companies to attract and retain the best talent. Companies that spent time on their core purpose, worked out their values, and crafted their vision while navigating through the turbulent times, came out on top.

The Desired State

Jim Collins created a Vision Framework[3] in 2002, and it is still relevant today. The two components, "Preserve the Core" and "Stimulate Progress," gave organizations the structure for stability to stay grounded yet be resilient while pursuing goals.

Collins emphasizes holding on to what drives your organization — the values and purpose — while fostering and encouraging growth. Any company that's not growing, in any sense, is stagnating. You can guess which type of situation employees prefer!

Core ideology is the rock on which the company stands, articulated through core values and core purpose. The envisioned future is defined using a "Big Hairy Audacious Goal" (BHAG) and a vivid vision statement. Although Collins mentioned a 10-30-year BHAG, almost no one attempts to go to 10 years these days; most use five — the pace of change is way too fast!

---

3   Collins, Jim. "Vision Framework." https://www.jimcollins.com/tools/vision-framework.pdf

Once the vision is complete, think of it as the highest level of a cascading framework:

Which is then brought to life by articulating the overall vision for the organization:

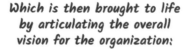

FIGURE 6-2
PRESERVE THE CORE/STIMULATE PROGRESS

Unless you've lived under a rock for a decade, you've heard of these concepts and maybe worked on them. They apply to any size company in all industries. If you've never had statements of purpose, vision, and values or haven't updated them in the past five years, it's time to overhaul them. Purpose, values, vision, and a BHAG define your desired state. Let's get started!

Core Ideology: Core Values — The First Step

Examples of core values on page 93 *were* from prior clients when I worked with them. Some have been updated and adjusted as they have evolved. In most cases, these appear on websites, are used in interview questions, are included in hiring guidelines and training manuals, and are reinforced during routine daily conversations. I do a **pop quiz** with all my leadership teams until they can reiterate these without looking at anything.

You'll see there's no prescribed way core values should look. It's up to the team to create a way of expressing core values that work for them.

Core Ideology: Core Purpose — The Second Step

In strategy, we also spend time understanding your "why," which is often referred to as your *purpose*. I push my clients to be thoughtful about "why" they do what they do. The first thing that comes to mind is usually "making a profit." Naturally, the reality is that every for-profit company wants to make a profit — you're not in business to lose money! However, your core purpose should be to drive deeper behaviors.

Company	Core Values
Partners In Change (Strategy Consulting)	Lifetime learners, Challenging the status quo, Feedback is a gift, Strategy is energizing & fun
Al Neyer (Design-Build/ Development)	We Take Ownership, We Dig the Details, We Build Relationships Through Trust, We Deliver Superior Service, We Run to Win & Stop to Celebrate
Matandy (Steel Processor)	***OWN IT*** We put **O**ur people and customers first We honor our **W**ord We **N**imbly solve problems We are **I**nnovative & embrace our entrepreneurial spirit We **T**ake responsibility for our actions & contributions
JBM Packaging (Packaging Company)	Collaboration, Grit, Growth, Growth Mindset, Innovation, Ownership, & Passion for a Better World
Process Plus Group (Engineering, Automation, & Construction)	Empowered Employees, Continuous Improvement, Teamwork & Collaboration, Problem Solving with Passion
Stober (Assembler/Distributor)	Seeking the best, Operating with integrity, Serving others, Growth through learning
Solid Blend (Water Management)	We're **Rapid Responders** who are committed to **Finding Win/Win Solutions**. We're **Curious** & committed to **Continuous Learning**. We're **Honest** & strive to be **Humble** & **Kind** in all we do.

Company	Purpose Statement
Partners In Change	To Be Your Sherpa — An Experienced Guide Helping Your Organization's Future
Al Neyer	Building Pride in Real Estate
Matandy	Matandy Steel is Helping Build America
JBM Packaging	Better Solutions. Better Lives. Better World.
Process Plus Group	Resolving Complex Issues for Our Customers
Stober	Deliver Peace of Mind in the Demanding World of Motion
Solid Blend	To Create an Environment Where the Team, Clients, & Community to Thrive

You'll see that on the previous page there are also some awesome purpose statements from a few of my clients.

Envisioned Future: Vision Statement and Vivid Description — The Third Step

In my experience, vision is the last thing to tackle. It takes several iterations and 18-36 months to nail your long-term vision.

This does not mean you don't do it for three years; you use draft statements to pursue what you have so far on a "that will do" basis. You want to wait to roll out the vision until the long-term picture of where you're going is clear.

Generally, strategic plans last for three years, so the vision solidifies at some point in the first cycle. Given that a vision is typically written for a 10-year period, you have at least two more strategic cycles before that vision gets accomplished. You should move forward with longer-term goals and the strategic priorities (Chapter 7) for the current cycle and continue to take the time to define your vision.

Here are vision statement examples from clients:

Company	Vision Statement
Partners In Change	100% Implementation of Their Strategies by Our Clients
Al Neyer	Dominate in Our Markets & Cities
Matandy	Excellence Today for a BETTER Tomorrow
JBM Packaging	Be the Role Model for a Sustainable, Purpose-Driven Company
Process Plus Group	To be the Firm of Choice, Delivering Exceptional Service Engaged Employees, Delivering Exceptional Services, Resulting in Enthusiastic Customers
Stober	STOBER Drives Will be Recognized as the Gold Standard
Solid Blend	Regional Leader in Healthcare for Clean Water

Pulling all this together requires the right people on the bus; the first time you do strategy, you may not yet have those people on board. After the first year of strategic planning, you will most likely need additions — a marketing person, maybe a CFO, IT person, etc. **Structure follows strategy, and key people's investment may be needed.** I'll cover this more in Chapter 10.

The second (and perhaps even the third) update is where you get a good idea of your desired state. The process gets easier, and you learn along the way; work the process for as long as it takes, hire the people you need to figure it out, and ultimately you will define and then execute on the vision.

Four Tips for Reaching Your Vision

"Building a visionary company requires 1% vision and 99% alignment."[4]

Research study after research study of New Year's resolutions indicates that more than 90% of people never actually achieve them; this can be true with company goals as well. **Vision without a plan is part of the reason why only 8% of us (the elite!) reach our goals; visioning alone is not the answer — you need a plan to support it.**

Consider these four tips for hitting your goals, achieving your vision, and living a life of purpose:

1. **Begin with the End in Mind:** Write it down, draw a picture, make it visible!
2. **Build a Support System:** Tell people, ask for help, find a mentor, and listen to advice.
3. **Set Specific Goals and "Stretch" Goals:** Research shows that specific and more challenging goals lead to higher performance 90% of the time — be clear and precise.

What? Not me! 4. **Recognize when you are procrastinating:** Set priorities, deadlines, and then focus.

Strategic planning is about choosing the path to do the hard work (resilience) to get to a better place (attain our vision and fulfill our purpose).

The Phases/Who Does What?

In the second part of **Phase 2: Plan Development**, you're going to define your desired state. You will:
- Create your core values, purpose, and vision.
- Make three-year strategic goals using a tool.
- Add the items above to your working draft of your strategic plan.

The Activities Overview

On page 96 you'll find the map for the team's activities for **Phase 2: Plan Development**.

---

4   Collins, Jim, and Jerry Porras. *Built to Last*. Harper Business, 1994.

Activity 1: Values, Purpose, and Vision. Use the exercises and tools to develop your values, purpose, and vision, including your 5-10-year BHAG.

Activity 2: Develop Your Three-Year Goals. Develop three-year goals to create your initial financial and strategic goals.

Activity 3: Complete Your Strategic Plan Summary. Use the Strategic Plan Summary Tool, adding your values, purpose, vision, and three-year goals.

Initiated by the Strategic planning team leader. Completed by the Strategic planning team, including Owners.

Every part of creating the desired state is a strategic planning team effort, although individuals can prepare their ideas before each meeting.

Activity 1: Values, Purpose, and Vision

This activity is the most intense, so I've split it into separate exercises.

Exercise 1: Core Values

These are essential characteristics that the organization should exhibit to create the best chance of success. Once you have them, they seldom change, but be aware that the timeframe for development is in the region of six to 12 months.

Guidelines for Core Values:

- A set of values and beliefs should guide every organization and be aggressively authentic.
- Provides an underlying framework for making decisions (who to hire, who to fire, which customers align to our values, and which do not).
- Values are often rooted in ethical themes — honesty, trust, integrity, respect, and fairness — but can also include market-facing values like innovation, creativity, thought leadership, etc.
- Values should apply to the entire organization.
- Should be more than a word or phrase — be ready to expand on it with a statement.

There are many ways to identify or create your core values. I like to have my clients start with the question, "Who would you take if you started a new office someplace else?" For example, the group could prepare with this homework:

- You are going to open a new office. You can take three people. Who would you take?
- Why would you take those people? Brainstorm core values that make these people successful team members.
- Share with your leadership team. Choose the ones that best define the successful behaviors you want to encourage.

Once the Strategic planning team has assembled a list of the core values, we sometimes use surveys, employee town halls, or one-on-one interviews to have employees supply feedback. The idea is to clarify and communicate the core values, namely the aggressively authentic behaviors that maximize success at your company. The goal is to have the wider employee group learn, understand your thoughts about culture, and provide feedback for whether they think each core value is a "fit."

Exercise 2: Core Purpose

The core purpose encapsulates why the organization exists — what its purpose is. Purpose is simple, concise, and emotional. It delivers a hook that guides leaders, motivates employees, and turns customers into lifelong fans. Once confirmed, it rarely changes and sits alongside the vision in terms of timeframe. If you have ever been to Disney, I bet you know their purpose is "to create happiness." Disney invests significant resources in their hiring and training program to help connect this to each employee.

If you have seven minutes, watch the Simon Sinek YouTube video "Start with Why" — or his longer talk (which is 18 minutes).

Your purpose should appeal to your and your employees' emotions! Make sure you share this throughout the organization.

Guidelines for Core Purpose:

- The essence of why the organization exists is based on who you are and what you do.
- Explains the basic needs you fulfill.
- Should be brief, to the point, and easy to understand.
- Ideally, it conveys your organization's unique nature and its unique role that differentiates you from others.

Exercise 3: Vision

Where do you want to be in five to 10 years? How do you define winning? What will you look like as an organization, and how would you know you'd made it? The answer comes in two parts. The first part is a vision statement, and the second is the measurable BHAG.

> **Guidelines for Vision:**
> - How the organization wants to be perceived in the future — what success looks like.
> - An expression of the desired end state.
> - Challenges everyone to reach for something significant — inspiring.
> - Provides long-term focus for the entire organization.

When it comes to vision, it's a good idea to start with the two parts and then expand the vision with areas that the company will work on and the bold steps it will take in the next three years. The vision framework below gives you the idea of how this might look:

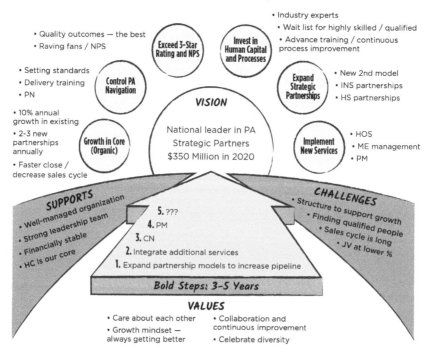

FIGURE 6-3C
VISION FRAMEWORK: 5-YEAR BOLD STEPS — CLIENT EXAMPLE

Within the vision, inside the rising sun, you place your vision phrase and potentially a big five- to 10-year goal in the center. At the bottom, your values are listed as bullets inside the arrow. I also like to add the purpose statement to this.

Around the vision sun are circles I like to call "themes." Modify them to match the areas you believe will support your success. Each theme will have its own actions and desired results to help you achieve your goal. My recommendation is to make these as measurable as possible to focus on the desired outcome of each. Below that are the bold steps you will make in the next three years to move you toward your vision.

Back to Jim Collins for a moment. He talked about "vivid descriptions;" he was clear that a vision needs a compelling medium — a way of "selling it" to make it come to life for your company. I suggest four ways of doing this:

Check out this video!

1. Create a picture, for example, a storyboard[5]
2. Write it as an article for a news story
3. Make a video describing your future
4. Develop a power-point with key parts of your vision and milestones

This is a critical responsibility of the strategic planning team. I give this as "homework" and allow each person on the strategic planning team to share their vision. I encourage them to tell their story using whatever framework they want. An example of an article might be:

It is 2030, and we have accomplished everything we wanted most. We have become so successful that a magazine featured us in this week's issue as its cover story. **What's featured on the cover? What are the major headlines and images? What are the sidebars and quotes? Remember, the story has *already* been written. If you can't recall the details, JUST MAKE IT UP!**

After each member of the strategic planning team shares their vision, the goal is to create one aligned version of the bold steps. The "work" is to develop shared themes across each person's vision. This encourages engagement and extreme ownership.

You won't be ready to share this with your whole company yet, but you will at least have inspired your key players and created a shared document.

Finally, reflect on how you've articulated your vision — you may have *several vision statements* that resonate with you or *themes* that will be very significant over time. Hold on to those — you'll need them for your strategic plan.

---

5 "Draw Your Future." *YouTube*, uploaded by ThisIsRealBusiness, 4 Jan. 2013, https://www.youtube.com/watch?v=A7KRSCyLqc4.

Activity 2: Develop Your Three-Year Goals

The final element of this phase of **Plan Development** is to work on your three-year goals, expressed as **key measures of success**. Where do you want your numbers to be, and what will success look like? Add other measures that are important to you.

3 Year Strategic Goals Date in 3 years	Key Measures of Success	What does this look like by 5-year Vision Themes
	Revenue: $42	Integrate Acquisitions
	Profit / EBITDA: 12%	• Fully integrated • New Div strategic in place?
	Other key Measures:	
	Customer Retention at >93%	Sales Focus • Expanded sales team model • 4 Jumbo/strategic clients
	Expansion: $2.5 (new business – product line) Acquisition: $5-$10M	• White label /institution product in place • Expanded channels (e-commerce in place)
	Productivity: 20% improvement over 3 years	
		Target Markets with Personal Services • Market focused service model • Enhanced service models with tiers/levels • Empower service model in place • 2 or 3 service locations (geographies) to cover time zones and expand labor market pool
		Invest in People and Process • Automatic workflow tools • New platform for ERP • Individual Development Plans in place with training • ESOP

FIGURE 6-4C
STRATEGIC PLAN SUMMARY: DESIRED STATE TOOL
— 3-YEAR STRATEGIC GOALS — CLIENT EXAMPLE

You have two sources to help you begin; both of these had at least a five-year outlook:

1. The Owner created the stakeholder goals in the first step of **Listen and Learn**.
2. The themes and BHAG you drafted as part of the vision in Exercise 3.

Use those as your starting point and work back to estimate where you need to be in three years to reach the five-year goals. This may take a while because each person on the strategic planning team should agree to the three-year measures of success. Most likely this will be stretch goals and will require changes to make them happen.

Activity 3: Complete Your Strategic Plan Summary

The section relating to the work in this chapter is shown on page 102 (Figure 6-5).

You already have your three-year strategic goals. All that remains is to complete the top three sections.

I thought it would be helpful for you to see "complete" desired states showing core values, purpose, vision, and some of key concepts. In Appendix 3 there are a couple of vision visuals these companies rolled out to their organization. → *Go take a look!*

Chapter Summary

In this chapter, you:
- Understood the importance of core values, purpose, and vision as part of your desired state.
- Learned the lifespan of these three components of your desired state.
- Distinguished purpose and vision as separate and different.
- Completed team exercises to help you develop or update values, purpose, and vision.
- Chose the BHAG to support your vision and allow you to complete the initial desired state.
- Developed three-year goals for your strategy.
- Updated your strategic plan summary.

STRATEGY *IN MOTION*
PLAN DEVELOPMENT

STRATEGIC PLAN
SUMMARY–
WORKING DRAFT

DESIRED STATE
(Purpose, Values, Vision, Goals)

Company Purpose	(The Why – why you do what you do)
Co. Core Values	The How – essential characteristics that define success in your organization)
Vision	(Desired State - where do you see the organization to be in 5-10 years) Vision Themes Vision statements (brainstorms) 10-year target:

3 Year Strategic Goals Date in 3 years	**Key Measures of Success**	**What does this look like by 5-year Vision Themes**
	Revenue: $	• Themes -what is in place
	Profit / EBITDA:	• Themes -what is in place
	Other key Measures:	• Themes -what is in place

+1 513.807.6647 | DARCY@STRETCH-SL.COM | STRETCH-SL.COM

FIGURE 6-5
STRATEGIC PLAN SUMMARY: DESIRED STATE TOOL
To download, visit stretch-sl.com/SIMtools or follow the QR code in the Preface

NOTES

NOTES

CHAPTER 7

Plan Development: Strategic Choices

"Strategy 101 is about choices: you can't be all things to all people."
—Michael Porter

The Power of Choice

In my marathon example, there were only two things I could spend time on while training: running and my graduate work. There was literally no space for anything else, and believe me, I tried. I had to say "no" to many things to have any chance of success. Oh, I did add in showering and eating!

Strategic planning is about *choices* and *priorities*. To be good at something, you can't do everything. I remind my clients that in order to win, you need to a "no" strategy.

Every client I've worked with struggles with saying "no," yet all of them tell me they want to be great at "something," which requires focus. There are customers and activities where your business is making money — say "yes" to these and "no" to those losing you money. Also, consider that there are some employees who helped you be successful today, but may not have the skills to reach the next level of growth.

To begin filtering where to say "no," I use the 80/20 Pareto Principle, which I have seen played out repeatedly. **For example, many times 80% of your revenue comes from 20% of your customers.** Is this true of your business? These accounts may or may not be profitable, by the way! Strategy is about choosing to focus on the most profitable and growing that part of your business to increase your bottom line.

Once you've made your choices, you focus on a 12-18-month timeframe by selecting the most important *priorities*.

In This Chapter

In this chapter, we're working on the final steps of the ***Plan Development Phase*** — **determine strategic choices** and **outline strategic priorities**.

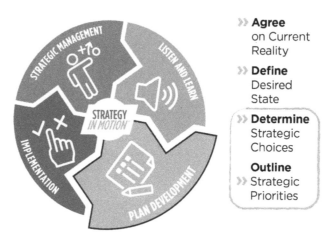

>> **Agree**
on Current
Reality

>> **Define**
Desired
State

>> **Determine**
Strategic
Choices

Outline
>> Strategic
Priorities

During this step of ***Phase 2: Plan Development***, you will make your directional choices for the next three years.

The key strategic questions you're trying to answer are:

1. What should we build/grow?
2. What should we hold/defend?
3. What should we divest/harvest?
4. Should we expand into new markets?
5. Should we grow with new products/services?

Recognizing the Messy Middle

We just discussed how one of the most challenging things for a small business to say is "no." These companies kicked and scratched their way through a Stage 1 business (Figure 1-3: The Evolution of Strategic Planning — "Meet Budget" section) and have lots of customers to prove it! Unfortunately, they add infrastructure, people, and cost along the way — and some have expanded their products and services, based on each customer's differing needs. The result is that they often get stuck because their business has become complicated, margins have decreased, and they are constrained by resources and/or cash.

Making good strategic choices is hard — that's why I call this the "messy middle." Here is how two of my clients described the messy middle:

> *"A series of choices you make that are going to push your company forward into the best it can be. Saying 'no' to things that aren't going to get you there."*

"A game plan to allocate resources to get the best possible outcome for your company. You need to figure out where you are making money and why — this must be done through an honest and realistic approach."

Companies who tackle the messy middle and create laser-focused offer(s) and target market(s), with a clear statement of what they will *not* do simply do better. I'll say that one more time, *companies who tackle the messy middle* **simply do better**.

Warning: Many companies will brainstorm their purpose, mission, core values, and vision, then jump straight to strategic priorities, **avoiding the messy middle choices of your target markets, customers, and products/services**. That may be all right the first time you do strategy, but the messy middle has a lot of **profit potential** if we dare to focus and say "no."

CASE STUDY

Water Treatment Plant

I worked with a water treatment company, with owners who invested in strategy and culture. When I started collaborating with them, they had a good foundation with a mission statement, values, and vision. During our first meeting, I saw a huge opportunity to identify a purpose, focus, and solve the messy middle.

Ken and his wife, the owners, were incredible community partners and had grown by supporting numerous small clients. As the company expanded, their cost to serve increased, and, unfortunately, many of their small clients were costing them more to support than they earned in income!

Their newly hired COO realized this — he created a spreadsheet to show that >80% of their revenue was the results of <20% of their customers.* The company had more than 1,000 clients for a 10-person staff, constraining the organization and leaving no room to focus on growth opportunities.

The strategic planning team edited the famous quote from Peter Drucker — they created a strategic priority called "Starve the Problems." They used this as the basis for allocating resources.

Their ideal clients were hospitals and health care systems needing water treatment — large accounts and, potentially, very profitable if grown and served well. **Working at *both* ends of the market is difficult for a small company; there are not enough resources to serve such a wide range of clients.**

We spent at least three meetings on "choices." Chris, the

COO, and Steve, from sales, saw an opportunity for a pricing strategy that implemented a minimum project cost. Gradually, they moved clients up to the minimum level, or they politely said no to the client. This was tough for the owners to do but critical to their strategy — hence Chris' quote: "Strategy can be Painful."

*The Pareto Principle says that 20% of input causes roughly 80% of the output. Vilfredo Pareto was an Italian economist who lived in the late 1890s and early 20th century. He investigated the distribution of wealth in Italy and found that roughly 20% of the population owned approximately 80% of the land. This "rule" ended up playing out in different populations he investigated. Though the Pareto Principle was not used for many years, others began to appreciate the concept, most notably: Peter Drucker, Harvard Professor George K. Zipf in his Principle of Least Effort,[1] and quality expert Joseph Juran's Rule of the Vital Few.

Not that you care... but it's interesting!

NOTE: The Principle of Least Effort is the theory that the "one primary principle" in any human action, including verbal communication, is the expenditure of the least effort to accomplish a task.

Dr. Joseph Juran was the first to point out that what Pareto and others had observed was a "universal" principle — one that applied in an astounding variety of situations, not just economic activity, and appeared to hold without exception in problems of quality.

Eventually, Pareto's Principle was proven repeatedly in a variety of situations — namely, 80% of results for just about anything comes from only 20% of the activity.

I have seen this demonstrated in companies in many contexts. For example:

REVENUE: 80% from 20% of your clients
PROFITS: 80% from 20% of your products/services
HR PROBLEMS: 80% from just 20% of your employees
COMPLAINTS: 80% from 20% of clients or people

It's a fundamental principle of competitive strategy: the secret of success is to concentrate your resources on your *strengths* and develop an advantage over the competition. It takes work to find where the rule applies in each business, and once identified, it becomes easier to say "no."

Grand strategies depend on a limited number of large opportuni-

1   The Principle of Least Effort (PLE) was proposed in 1949 by Harvard linguist George Kingsley Zipf in *Human Behavior and the Principle of Least Effort.*

ties. This means taking advantage of current niches for a small business, namely the markets/customers you already serve well and the products and services you already offer. You need to consider a fundamental question: *Where are you making money, and where are you losing money?* Pareto's 80/20 Principle typically shows islands of profitability hiding inside an unprofitable business. I encourage my clients start with uncovering opportunities in their existing business, first. These will be less risky and, potentially, faster to build.

Successfully executing on strategy requires tough, uncomfortable choices based on simple logic and solid principles. It is necessary to challenge how you think about who you serve and what you offer.

The Driving Force

A business can plot its product/service *direction* with the next tool, the Ansoff Matrix.[2] Companies love to explore every opportunity, so they try and complete the whole matrix; that's a great place to start. The purpose is to consider the strategy for if and when company a should venture into new area — a product extension, an additional service, a new market, etc. Expanding to "New Products" or "New Markets" takes significant resources, specific competencies, and more time than you think! Unfortunately, I have seen many of my clients try to do both directions at once, which is also very costly.

The Ansoff Matrix, often called the Growth Matrix, is shown to the left. Your market/product opportunities will be in one of these boxes.

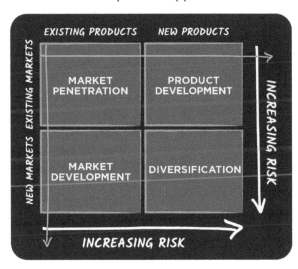

FIGURE 7-1
ANSOFF MATRIX

This task is one where I often have to have hard conversations. For small businesses especially, the reality is that they are constrained by cash and resources, so they need to choose. **It doesn't mean "never," it just means to prioritize.** I highly encourage most clients to stay away from the

2   Created by Igor Ansoff, applied mathematician and business manager.

"Diversification" quadrant unless absolutely necessary. In fact, I call it the "D for Dumb" box!

The **yellow arrows** on the grid relate to a **driving force**.[3] I have simplified this to two distinct directional "choices," which works for about 80% of my clients:

1. **"Market-Served" Driving Force** (vertical arrow): involves simplifying your current customers down to a couple of key markets or "niches" — this encourages focus so you can decide how best to serve the market. The water treatment company mentioned earlier was moving in this direction and focused on two complementary healthcare markets: (1) Hospitals; and (2) Assisted Living. Their strategy was to find solutions to manage these markets best and bundle value-added services. Over time, this strategy may involve product and service development as you find new ways to add value to your current segments.

2. **"Products-Offered" Driving Force** (horizontal arrow): involves simplifying your products/services into a couple of core offerings. My company is a good example. I do strategic planning as my primary "product." Although my client base is diverse, strategy is my core product 80% of the time, and I *customize* it for each customer/market. I spend much of my time in "market development," marketing strategy, and finding key relationships/ collaborators to help.

Remember, you need to clean up your existing business before adding anything new. Gino Wickman[4] writes about how CEOs love "shiny new things." I was listening to the book with my son, Logan, in the car, and when he heard that line, he looked at me and asked, "Mom, is that true? **Do CEOs really like shiny new objects?** That sounds so weird." I sadly replied, "Yep, sometimes to the downfall of their current business."

Owners will buy machines, but not invest in marketing!

It amazes me how a business may make a large investment in a new piece of equipment but then wince at training for current employees or spending money on marketing their current products. According to Harvard Business School professor Clayton Christensen, there are over 30,000 products introduced every year, and 95% fail.[5] **That doesn't mean you shouldn't pursue them — it just means you need to take the time to do it right and recognize it will take longer than you think.**

In my experience, companies want to do everything! They are afraid to eliminate existing business, including unprofitable clients or prod-

3 Freedman, Mike, and Benjamin Tregoe. *The Art and Discipline of Strategic Leadership*. McGraw Hill, 2004.
4 Wickman, Gino. *Traction*. BenBella Books, 2012.
5 Christensen, Clayton. "95 Percent of New Products Fail. Here Are 6 Steps to Make Sure Yours Don't." Inc, https://www.inc.com/marc-emmer/95-percent-of-new-products-fail-here-are-6-steps-to-make-sure-yours-dont.html.

ucts. Somehow, they think they can continue adding new things — new markets, new products, and new services. Their resources are over-stretched, and as we hear daily, they run out of cash, which is why many small businesses do not make it. The reality is you need to do less, so you can do more. Resource — including cash — management is critical for a small business, especially in a growth phase.

The messy middle can be complicated and involves some trial and error. If you are tempted to get into the weeds, focus on your strengths and the largest sources of revenue. Find your key market segments by focusing on your top 20% of accounts, which make up 80% of your revenue. You can clean up the rest with an appropriate pricing plan — more on that in Chapter 10.

The Phases/Who Does What?

As we just discussed, in **Plan Development**, you will **determine strategic choices** and **outline strategic priorities**. You will:
- Choose where to:
  - Build/grow
  - Hold/defend
  - Divest/harvest
  - Grow with new markets
  - Grow with new products/services
- Create three-year strategic choices
- Develop your choices into approximately one-year strategic priorities
- Add the items above to your working draft of your strategic plan

The Activities Overview

Here's the map for the team's activity for the final two parts of **Phase 2: Plan Development**:

Activity 1: Business Segmentation. Use the Business Segmentation Tool with the help of your CFO/Controller and sales leader to identify where you want to be with your markets and products/services in three years.

Activity 2: Market and Product Strategy. Use the Ansoff Matrix to brainstorm new markets and products/services.

Activity 3: Law of Attractiveness. Use the Rating Tool to assess the viability of your analysis from Steps 1 and 2. Define your strategic choices.

Activity 4: Strategic Priorities. Develop your strategic priorities that will, over the next 12-18 months, make a start on progressing toward your three-year goals. Complete a Strategic Priority Plan Tool for up to three priorities.

Activity 5: Key Choices to Close the Gap. Complete the Pre-Plan Tool: Business Segmentation with your strategy and investment plans.

Initiated by the strategic planning team leader. Completed by the strategic planning team, with department heads and executive approval.

Activity 1: Business Segmentation

Let me first highlight, this is an advanced-planning tool and takes commitment to complete. You may be limited by how you collect the data, and it may take a few times to get it right. Once complete, the Pre-Plan Tool: Business Segmentation (Figure 7-2 on page 113) helps you understand business segments: the intersection of your key markets and offerings (products *and* services). It takes work to define your markets (industry, size of client, geography, etc.), and you need to pull your products/services apart to see where their true value is.

The key is to define your markets separately from your products and services. This can be difficult for many first-time planners. Some of the complication is the internal accounting system. It takes a few times to determine the best way to set up this matrix for the next step. This tool will help you prioritize, decide how much to invest, determine whether or not to divest, and make strategic choices.

At the end of Activity 1 on page 114, there is an example of this tool from a small architecture company (Figure 7-2C).

CASE STUDY

Market Served Driving Force

When this architecture company first completed the Business Segmentation Tool, they identified over 12 different markets based on their customers. Architecture services, alone, were becoming a commodity and they needed to find areas to increase profit by adding more value. **The company made a key hire who brought with them the ability to expand into a key profitable product (OF) to their current markets.** Not every market saw this value. They decided to focus their resources on a few

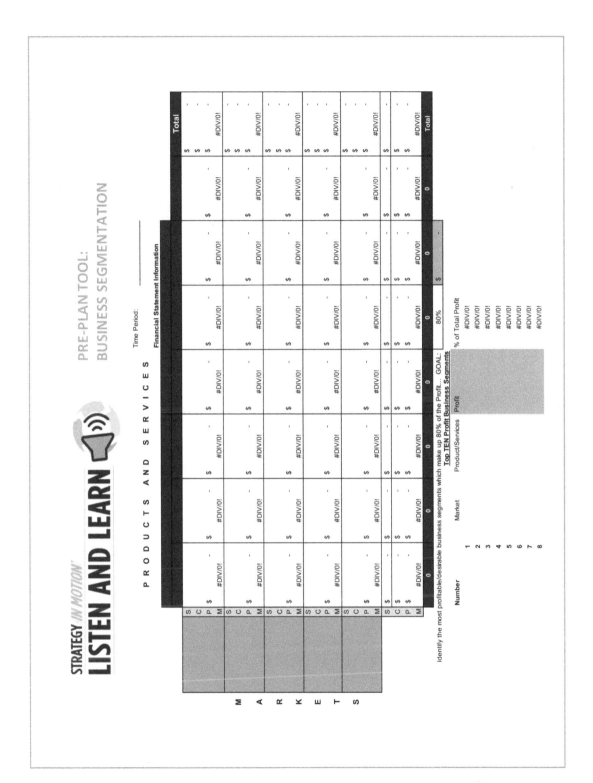

FIGURE 7-2
PRE-PLAN TOOL: BUSINESS SEGMENTATION
To download, visit stretch-sl.com/SIMtools or follow the QR code in the Preface

target markets and reduced their effort to serve the others. Over time, they added market leaders to drive revenue and find new clients. This is a "market served" driving force. This can be a great strategy for small businesses, but many times it requires saying "no" and implementing key hires with the skill sets you need.

				Design	Studies	CD	OF	Total
M A R K E T	Commercial	Office	S	$ 175,000.00		$ 100,000.00	$ 20,000.00	$ 295,000.00
			C	$ 160,000.00		$ 93,000.00	$ 14,000.00	$ 267,000.00
			P	$ 15,000.00	$ -	$ 7,000.00	$ 6,000.00	$ 28,000.00
			M	8.57%		7.00%	30.00%	9.49%
		Retail	S	$ 45,000.00		$ 34,000.00		$ 79,000.00
			C	$ 32,000.00		$ 32,000.00		$ 64,000.00
			P	$ 13,000.00	$ -	$ 2,000.00	$ -	$ 15,000.00
			M	28.89%		5.88%		18.99%
	Housing	Single	S	$ 160,000.00	$ 15,000.00			$ 175,000.00
			C	$ 156,000.00	$ 12,500.00			$ 168,500.00
			P	$ 4,000.00	$ 2,500.00	$ -	$ -	$ 6,500.00
			M	2.50%	16.67%			3.71%
		MTF	S	$ 35,000.00			$ 30,000.00	$ 65,000.00
			C	$ 29,000.00			$ 25,000.00	$ 54,000.00
			P	$ 6,000.00	$ -	$ -	$ 5,000.00	$ 11,000.00
			M	17.14%			16.67%	16.92%
	Other		S		$ 14,000.00		$ 15,000.00	$ 29,000.00
			C		$ 12,000.00		$ 12,500.00	$ 24,500.00
			P	$ -	$ 2,000.00	$ -	$ 2,500.00	$ 4,500.00
			M		14.29%		16.67%	15.52%
			S	$ 415,000.00	$ 29,000.00	$ 134,000.00	$ 65,000.00	$ 643,000.00
			C	$ 377,000.00	$ 24,500.00	$ 125,000.00	$ 51,500.00	$ 578,000.00
			P	$ 38,000.00	$ 4,500.00	$ 9,000.00	$ 13,500.00	$ 65,000.00
			M	9.16%	15.52%	6.72%	20.77%	10.11%

Design	Studies	CD	OF	Total
		GOAL:	80%	$ 52,000.00

Top TEN Profit Business Segments

Number	Market (Major)	Sub	Product/Services	Profit	% of Total Profit
1	Commercial	Office	Design	$ 15,000.00	23%
2	Commercial	Retail	Design	$ 13,000.00	20%
3	Commercial	Office	CD	$ 7,000.00	11%
4	Commercial	Office	Int Des	$ 6,000.00	9%
5	Housing	NFP	Design	$ 6,000.00	9%
6	Housing	NFP	Int Des	$ 5,000.00	8%
7	Housing	FT	Design	$ 4,000.00	6%

FIGURE 7-2C

PRE-PLAN TOOL: BUSINESS SEGMENTATION — CLIENT EXAMPLE

Activity 2: Market and Product Strategy

Now let's consider some of key opportunities from your SWOT to analyze all market/offering expansion plans using the Ansoff Matrix.

Our water treatment company heard from customers during **Listen and Learn** that they would appreciate emergency service rather than the 7am to 5pm window that was currently being offered. They decided to create an emergency service offering, targeting markets to support with additional vehicles and staff. *FYI, they also made a key hire!*

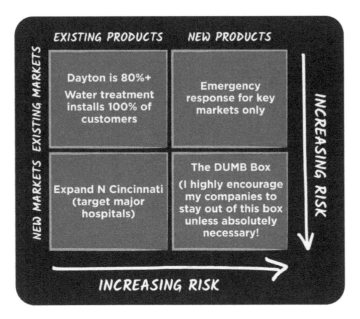

FIGURE 7-3C
ANSOFF MATRIX — CLIENT EXAMPLE

They also saw an opportunity to take their existing products to the Northern Cincinnati market, where there are several large hospitals.

Many of my clients plot their opportunities using the Ansoff Matrix. See the example above (Figure 7-3C).

Now it's time to close in on what would be optimal in terms of strategy and investment.

Activity 3: The Law of Attractiveness

When developing their original strategy, our water treatment company served several distinct types of organizations, with over 50% of their business revenue coming from a wide variety of clients. A spread of clients is tough for a small company to sustain *while in growth mode*. Critically, for a small company, you'll need to answer a tough question: *How attractive is each market segment (and/or customer) to our company?*

The first task is to develop the attractiveness criteria that you will use to assess optimal markets/customers using the current customer types as a guide.

First, you'll choose criteria against which to test the segment. Brainstorm and select three or four "Attractive Criteria:"

- **Growth rate** of segment
- Customer **bargaining power**
- Your **cost of serving** the segment

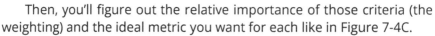

- Customer **price sensitivity**
- Segment **margin**
- Segment **sales volume**
- **Competition**

Then, you'll figure out the relative importance of those criteria (the weighting) and the ideal metric you want for each like in Figure 7-4C.

For the selected three criteria:

- "Growth" is the overall growth rate of the market segment. For example, the water treatment company listed "hospitals" as an important segment, and it's one they wanted to grow.
- "Margin" is the gross margin you want to make on your sale (**gross margin equals revenue minus cost of goods sold**); note that this is the highest weighted item.

Criteria	Weighting	Ideal
Growth	30%	>15%
Margin	40%	>30%
Competition	30%	Low

**FIGURE 7-4C
BUSINESS SEGMENT
ATTRACTIVENESS CRITERIA —
CLIENT EXAMPLE**

- "Competition" is a measure of how hard you'll have to fight for the sale.

Next, you create your scoring matrix:[6]

Criteria	Weight	1	2	3	4	5
Growth of Segment	35%	0-5%	5-10%	10-15%	15-20%	>20%
Gross Margin	30%	<20%	20-30%	30-40%	40-50%	>50%
Our Position *(Can we win)*	20%	Bottom	Low	Middle of Pack	Top 4	First Choice
Competition	15%	V High	High	Moderate	Low	None
Others	--					
Total	100%					

**FIGURE 7-5C
BUSINESS SEGMENT SCORING MATRIX — CLIENT EXAMPLE**

---

6   Modified from Matthews, Bill. *The 5-Ps to a Wow Business*. Sound Wisdom, 2018.

Before you can complete the rating table, you will need to research:
- The growth percentage for each segment
- The gross margin that your sales make in each segment
- The level of competition you face in this segment

Finally, you can score your market segments and compare them to each other:

Business Segement	Growth	Gross Margin	Our Position	Compe-tition	Rating	Invest Strategy
Hospitals	4	3	4	3	3.5	Build
Assisted Living	5	3	2	1	3.2	Hold
Contractors	2	2	3	2	2.7	Divest

FIGURE 7-6C
BUSINESS SEGMENT ATTRACTIVENESS — CLIENT EXAMPLE

For each row, columns two through four, multiply the criterion (e.g., growth) by its weighting (from the "weight" column in the scoring matrix in Figure 7-5C), then all three scores are added together in the "rating" column.

The initial instinct to lower the percentage of revenue from contractors was a good one. That doesn't mean firing clients (although it might), but rather that growth in the other two areas should outpace the less profitable one. In the event, they decided to divest by focusing on a key profitably relationships.

Strategy and Investment

Returning to the water treatment examples, their investment strategy for the next three years (Figure 7-7C) can be found on page 118.

On page 119 is a template (Figure 7-8) that will show you how to think about your market and product/service choices over the years. This should be done at a very high level and show the shifts in your business segments. This helps the organization know what is going to be different as we grow.

They completed their strategy for existing & new ventures.

They captured the resources they'd need to execute the strategy.

Choices	Today (% of Revenue)	+3 Years (% of Revenue)	Strategy	Resources (1st Year Investment)
Markets/ Customers	Hospitals: 10%	Hospitals: 40%	Grow *INVEST*	Add sales & marketing focus
	Assisted living: 10%	Assisted living: 20%	Hold *EXPAND OVER TIME*	Sales on targeted systems
	Contractors: 30%	Contractors: <15%	Divest	Focus on key accounts
	Remainder: 50%	Remainder: <25% — Focus on accounts that meet our criteria	Harvest SAY "NO" WHEN NEEDED	Increase price/ decrease services
Products/ Services	Water treatment	Add services for key markets — Emergency Service	Build/grow *INVEST*	Marketing & systems mapping
Geographies	Dayton — >80%	Expand N. Cincinnati (target major hospitals)	Build/grow *INVEST*	Add sales & determine how to support

FIGURE 7-7C
BUSINESS SEGMENT SCORING MATRIX — CLIENT EXAMPLE

Activity 4: Strategic Priorities

Now is it time to pull all the information together and determine your key Strategic Priorities, you identify the issues (make or breaks) that will be your focus for strategic activities for the next year or two. Over the past twenty years, I have seen companies set themselves up for failure, just because the pick "too many" strategic priorities. **My recommendation is to prioritize the list to three key changes, complete these, and then pick the next ones!**

To start, go back to your SWOT and consider your top three items in each quadrant. Also look at your vision and three-year goals. What are the critical areas to address and solve to move to our desired state? This will take some discussion and focus. List up to three strategic priorities and brainstorm the outcomes, or **SMART goals** (**S**pecific, **M**easurable, **A**chievable, **R**ealistic, and **T**angible/Time-specific). Remember, execution is hard, and I can tell you from experience — try to keep it to three!

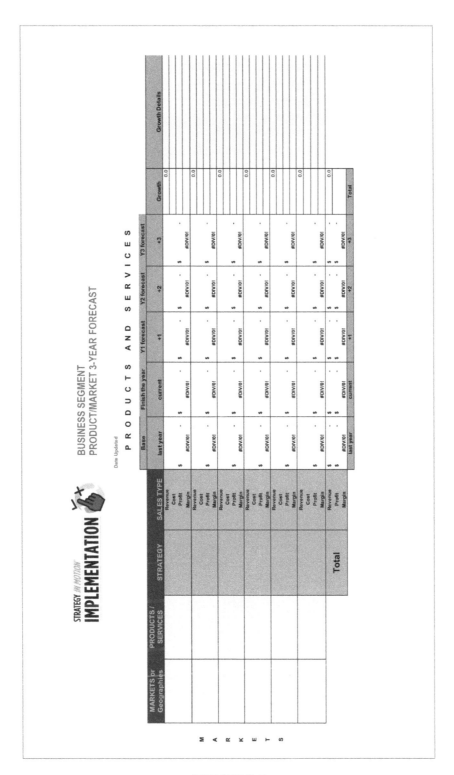

FIGURE 7-8
BUSINESS SEGMENTATION FORECAST TOOL
To download, visit stretch-sl.com/SIMtools or follow the QR code in the Preface

It is critical to choose your champion for each priority. This person should currently be on the strategic planning team and be willing to drive this priority. Also, discuss the four to five people who will be part of each of the strategic priority teams. You will expand the group to include key people in the organization who may not be in the strategic planning team. I encourage my companies to "double strategic capacity" at this point and choose additional priority team members to engage in developing the strategic priority plans.

Update your strategic plan with up to three strategic priorities:

1-2 year Strategic Priorities (make or breaks to address strategic issues and achieve the vision)	Strategic Priorities (champion, team)	12-18 Outcomes (SMART Goals / Key Projects)
	Invest in People Micha / Lucy, Sean, Joel, Seth	-Mentors for 70% of the organization -All New hires through formal Onboarding system -Improve retention to >75% for 0-3-years -Monthly Balanced Leadership KPIs with owners **Key Projects:** -Strategic Plan rollout (Marketing) -Structure and Roles to support growth (MT) -Identify and develop Role Descriptions for key hires (DB)
	Playbook 2.0 Chris / Anthony, Dan, Jamie	-Playbook Built with TOC and timing -50% of modules done with KPIs in place -SKU understanding and management **Key Projects:** -Database improvement (ERP / CRM Solution) -Operation Process mapping (CB) -Quality, Delivery, and Customer Relationship modules complete (Champions)
	Robust Balanced Product Roadmap Ryan / Joshua, Pete, Daniel, Molly	-Rollout 2 new products by end of the year -New Product KPIs and targets -R&D visits key customers / trade shows annually -Sustainable solution in 12 months **Key Projects:** -Product Development Process and Team (RB) -Fast-track business plan (MD) -Marketing and Sales alignment (DM)

FIGURE 7-9C
STRATEGIC PLAN SUMMARY: STRATEGIC PRIORITIES —
CLIENT EXAMPLE

Once you have your champion and your strategic priority teams, you expand on each of your priorities using the Strategic Priority Tool (Figure 7-10 on page 121).

Activity 5: Key Choices to Close the Gap

The last concept you need to understand is how to compete. The key is determining your "Strategic Competency" that best fits how you will win

STRATEGIC PRIORITY

Strategic Priority:		Date:	
Champion (sponsor of Priority):		Revision:	
Team (people responsible to deliver priority):			
Background (why is this a strategic issue and critical for the organizational focus			
Objectives and Outcome (s) *(what does success look like)*	*SMART Goals - Specific, Measurable, Attainable, Realistic, Tangible*		

Strategies - Key Initiatives/Projects (what are the big pictures activities to make the priority successful):

Strategy Key Initiative/Project	Project Owner / Project Team	Start Date	End Date	Cost	Measurement

Additional comments:

Possible Barriers (challenges/issues/concerns to meeting the results and completing initiatives. What may get in the way, i.e. Resources, buy-in, training, etc.):

What may get in the way?	What can we do to avoid this?	What do we do if it happens?

Resources (what do you need to make this happen):

Who do you need to help?	What do you need to spend money on?	Additional Comments

+1 513.807.6647 | DARCY@STRETCH-SL.COM | STRETCH-SL.COM

FIGURE 7-10
PLAN DEVELOPMENT: STRATEGIC PRIORITY TOOL
To download, visit stretch-sl.com/SIMtools or follow the QR code in the Preface

STRATEGY *IN MOTION*
PLAN DEVELOPMENT

STRATEGIC PLAN SUMMARY– WORKING DRAFT

STRATEGIC CHOICES
(Key Focus Areas and Investment Strategies)

Business Definition / Core Focus	(What specifically does your company do and for whom, consider your where you should win)

Strategic Choices: Core Markets / Offerings (Marketing Strategy)	**Key (Target) Markets (where should we focus to win)**	**Key Products/Services (how will our offerings change)**
	Right Fit Client (Criteria to define our Ideal Customer)	

Strategic (Core) Competency	(Your Strategic Differentiator(s), what makes you unique/different, What is your Measurable Brand Promise)

1-2 year Strategic Priorities (make or breaks to address strategic issues and achieve the vision)	**Strategic Priorities**	**Outcomes (SMART Goals)**

STRATEGIC BUDGET
(What are the Expectations for Plan Delivery?)

*Strategic Budget (agreed upon expectations for this plan to deliver)		Base year	+1	+2	+3	+4	+5
	Revenue						
	% Target Market						
	Margin						
	Productivity						
	Cash Flow						
	ROE						
	Others…						

Track key assumptions for strategic budget.

+1 513.807.6647 | DARCY@STRETCH-SL.COM | STRETCH-SL.COM

FIGURE 7-11
STRATEGIC PLAN SUMMARY: STRATEGIC CHOICES TOOL
To download, visit stretch-sl.com/SIMtools or follow the QR code in the Preface

with your target customers and markets. I cover this quite a bit in Chapter 10, but for now, consider Michael Porter's three main ways to compete:

- **Cost Leadership Strategy**: When you are in broad market and the market does not perceive you as unique. This is about being the low-cost choice. If your customers are focused on price, you need to be the lowest cost to win. This is difficult for small- to mid-size companies, but not impossible. Examples of cost leadership companies include Aldi, IKEA, and Walmart.
- **Differentiation Strategy**: When you are in a broad market and want to be unique. You need a strong brand, breakthrough marketing, plus a deep understanding of your customers, competitors, and what attributes make you unique: functions/features, quality/reliability, and/or convenience. There will be more on this in Chapter 10. Examples of companies with this strategy include Starbucks, Apple, and Chick-fil-a.
- **Niche Strategy**: When you target a group of customers with similar needs and focus on serving their needs. An example is landscape companies who focus on apartments. This can be a powerful strategy and typically involves geographic expansion to grow and/or add services or products to cross-sell to your niche market.

Now you are ready to update your Strategic Plan Summary: Strategic Choices Tool (Figure 7-11 on page 122). The working draft of your strategic plan is complete! Remember, it doesn't have to be perfect, but we don't have to get stuck either. In Chapter 8, we will move on to **Phase 3: Implementation**!

Chapter Summary

In this chapter, you:
- Learned that saying "yes" all the time is not a strategy.
- Reviewed choice as a powerful tool for focusing your business activities and deciding your direction.
- Understood the messy middle and how important it is to make decisions on where to invest and not invest.
- Used the Pareto Principle (80/20) to focus on the most productive areas of your business.
- Reviewed the Business Segmentation Tool and the Ansoff Matrix as ways to help you quantify your market and product/service goals and define your investment strategy.
- Defined 12–18-month strategic priorities.
- Updated your strategic plan summary.

NOTES

STRATEGY IN MOTION™

PHASE 3: Implementation

CHAPTER 8

Implementation

> **"We overestimate what we can do in one year, and underestimate what we can do in ten years."**
> —Bill Gates

Push to Action

This is the point where the rubber meets the road. Few companies stall in strategic planning, but many get stuck in the **Implementation** phase. Here are some general statistics to consider:

- 67% of companies fail at implementation.
- Less than 12% of companies meet monthly on strategy and track progress.
- As a result, less than 10% of companies successfully implement their strategic plan.

Having a plan is helpful — your leadership team took time to assess and develop a thoughtful plan. If you had good discussions with team alignment, you will be okay with the more manageable goals and activities (those that don't require a lot of change).

In my experience, the more challenging goals will require additional focus and time on implementation, or they won't happen. Cyndi Wineinger, my organizational development partner, says we have three choices: *freeze, flight,* or *fight*.

With your completed strategic plan in hand, you're probably itching to move toward your vision and BHAG. Don't give up and put it on the shelf *(flight)*. Many business owners get nervous and *freeze*. Your strategy will never be perfect, because we are predicting the future and you can't control it. Trust the process and recognize that key decisions will be assessed and updated along the way. **Planning is easy, but implementation is hard, so you must be ready to *fight*, so you don't get *stuck*.**

In This Chapter

>> **Create**
Scorecards &
Action Plans

>> **Update**
Structure

>> **Link** to Teams

>> **Communicate**
to Organization

Here is the good news: there IS a playbook for implementation. In this chapter, we'll build an implementation plan that will focus on the details, communication plans, and activities to implement your strategy successfully.

In this chapter, you will work with tools to help you create your implementation plan for the next 12-18 months.

The key strategic questions you're trying to answer are:

How will our strategic priorities progress across the one-year timeframe?
How will we know we're on track with our priorities?
What are things about our organization that might need to change?
How will we communicate our strategy to the company?

Leading Implementation

It's your job as a leadership team to define success (how to win), and then communicate, communicate, and communicate. Yes, I did mean to say "communicate" three times. You need to add the details and share it with others. Make your plan clear and simple — don't do a *Dilbert* on it![1]

A client of mine expressed their **Implementation** experience perfectly in this diagram:

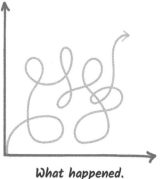

What I planned...   *What happened.*

In 2022, my son Logan co-lead the Leukemia & Lymphoma Society's Student of the Year campaign. As you probably know, co-leading is hard, especially if you don't have shared goals. This was a stretch for him and perfect for his high school challenge project. He set a goal to raise $25,000. He had a team of friends but no real role, clarity, or accountability.

Long story, short... about halfway through the campaign the team was at $4,000 and Logan was the only one feeling deflated. It was right before their 3V3 basketball tournament, and they had five people registered... not good! He was stuck.

It was time for the talk. I said, "Logan, if you want different results, you need to do different things. It's time to lead."

Fast forward, he took on more of the team leadership responsibilities and changed his approach. His co-leader, Daniel, focused on communication and was great at it. Logan started one-on-one conversations with each team member, set-up clear responsibilities, and put a "team" challenge in place: **If the team raised $5,000 in one week, he would shave his head.** *Guess what? This was the turning point. The team rallied behind his leadership and finished the campaign with $28,109.92. Nailed it!*

It Gets Easier with Practice

Many of my clients are "start from scratchers," and it can take a couple of tries to get a long-term strategic plan in place. You completed the critical parts, and you have a plan. If you worked the process thoroughly, you aligned on a few key assumptions, drafted purpose, values, vision, and goals, determined your strategic choices, and identified the key focus areas to change (namely, your strategic priorities).

Unfortunately, just when it's time to implement, many owners really do *freeze*. Some even *fly*, and head on vacation before there's time to communicate the plan, then return and forget they even had a plan! Yes, this happened — and, unfortunately, more than once.

CASE STUDY

School Products Company

I had the pleasure of working with a very innovative leadership team. Another outside consultant guided the company through a strategic process — they had a 20-page binder on the shelf to prove it. Unfortunately, there were so many recommendations that it was hard to know where to start. Additionally, the owner had just expanded his leadership team and saw little buy-in for the plan from his new team.

The first step was to audit the process and become familiar with current documents. I now call this, the Strategic Assessment, because people don't like the word audit...sorry all the accountants out there. They agreed to a few critical follow-ups and created a process focused on segmenting products and markets by revenue and profit, having a written strategic summary document with future key assumptions, developing strategic and operational scorecards, establishing a strategic leadership team with weekly meetings, and creating a communication plan with strategic updates.

What was remarkable about this company was how capable the leadership team was. The owner recognized the need to identify a president of the core business. Once in place, this person was very experienced at implementation and pulled information together and quickly developed scorecards to get things moving; one scorecard was focused on strategy, and the other on running the business. He put an operational team in place and reviewed the "Run-the-Business" scorecard monthly. This focus from the operations team created bandwidth for the leadership team to work on strategy.

This company was committed to implementation, developing action plans and scorecards (needed for a disciplined approach), and engaging additional people. Over the next two years, I met with the strategic team quarterly, and we completed a thorough update for year two. **It took patience, hard work, and communication.**

Seeing their progress with each update was impressive!

Winning companies have strategic thinking as part of their culture. To succeed long-term, you must get your current business under control first and then focus on what you wish to accomplish longer-term. It is tough to plan successfully when you are overwhelmed with daily fire-fighting activities. Many first-time planners use the first phase of strategic planning to address and solve critical operational issues and to develop strategic thinkers so they can then focus on long-term strategic changes.

Why Plans Fail

Plans fail for many reasons:
- Lack of a communication
- Plan after the strategy is developed
- Lack of an implementation plan and accountability
- Little buy-in and commitment from employees
- Doing the same thing and expecting different results
- Ignoring "business-based" realities
- Low or inappropriate resource allocation
- Basing decisions *only* on short-term budgets
- Multiple distractions

My goal is to give you the concepts and tools to continue to move forward and succeed — your strategy will improve with each update.

Don't Get Stuck

Why do so many companies get stuck in the *Implementation* phase? There are four main reasons:
1. **The leadership team waits for "perfection."** This is like the *freeze* mentioned above. Every question must be answered, every "i" dotted, and "t" crossed. Unfortunately, perfection will never happen because this is a forward-looking strategy, and we don't know what the future holds. We need to let go of "perfec-

tion" and go with "improvement." The strategy is our best guess with the information we currently have; as we get new information, we adjust. I want you to think about strategy as a process, and even better, an improvement process! It is a proactive way to keep the company focused on managing opportunities and threats versus reactive firefighting.

2. **The leadership is scared of being wrong.** Guess what, you will be! The best leaders take risks, are vulnerable, and recognize that they may make mistakes. Your strategy will be *more right* with each experience and piece of data. Remember, "You miss 100% of the shots you never take." The key is tracking, assessing, and updating.

3. **The leadership thinks it is only "their" job.** So, why tell or involve anyone? As we have seen, the strategic plan starts with leadership and the plan will impact the whole organization. The leadership team is responsible for providing and communicating a long-term vision and strategic plan for the company. Engaging and involving the organization is critical because they are vital to implementation. Once a strategic plan is done, one of the most complex parts is communicating and aligning the organization to support and follow through on the actions needed to reach the goal. Also, don't forget to celebrate successes; build an incentives and celebrations plan that aligns with your culture.

> 20% of leadership time should be spent on strategy and building a healthy culture. Many leaders spend only 5%.

4. **Good ideas alone won't cut it.** During planning, strategic priorities should have goals that pass the SMART test: Specific, Measurable, Attainable, Relevant, and Tangible/Time-specific. Organizations struggle with accountability because goals are unclear, and action plans are poorly documented or understood. The most successful strategic plans tie specific activities necessary to achieve the goal to the strategy execution teams and whoever is responsible for completing the tasks and managing the timeline. As Molly, a CEO for a design-build company, reminded me, "You need to be able to stick to a plan. Discipline is essential."

My vision for my clients is 100% implementation — specifically, for the high-level strategic priorities. Progress needs to be reviewed, tracked, and updated; how are your actuals tracking to your targets?

I recommend clients include monthly meetings and quarterly reviews for their strategic goals once they start **Implementation**. If you have a board, they are often too focused on operational issues, which may not be the best use of their time — the strategy should become their primary focus and area of support. I include a board meeting with each of my clients when we finish the plans. This helps hold the leadership team accountable to the strategy.

Where to Start

I recommend, at most, *three* strategic priorities for the next year; **keep an eye on the number *three* — it keeps coming up. The Rule of Three.**

Companies that invest in their people and teach employees to be strategic by involving them in implementation create a strategic-thinking culture. Without this participation, your people will not have the chance to engage more fully or develop their full potential. The bottom line is that growth will be inhibited.

The leadership team needs to do three things during this transition; *lead* (new people into the strategy circle), *coach* (up-and-coming employees), and *do* (the work of leadership).

Let's see how this all comes together.

The Phases/Who Does What?

In **Phase 3: Implementation**, there are four parts:
- Create scorecards and plans
- Update structure
- Link teams
- Communicate to organization

In this next section, you will:
- Complete your Implementation Checklist Tool. It ensures you don't miss anything.
- Set SMART goals to ensure alignment to key outcomes.
- Restructure how you manage strategy vs the day-to-day. Make sure you have the right people in the right seats. Hire new people if necessary.
- Update your executive, strategic, and operational teams.
- Prepare and execute on communicating your strategy and get buy-in to implement.

The Activities Overview

Here's the map for the team's activity for ***Implementation***:

Activity 1: Complete Your Implementation Checklist
Activity 2: Create Your Scorecards and Actions Plans
Activity 3: Optimize Your Leadership Teams
Activity 4: Plan Who Will Communicate the Strategy and How.
Determine what employees want to hear it and how to keep them updated. Ensure there are incentives and celebrations for reaching key objectives, milestones, and goals.

*Initiated by the strategic planning team leader. Completed by the strategic planning team. **In addition:** During **Implementation**, you will need help from finance, departmental heads, marketing, and HR.*

Activity 1: Complete Your Implementation Checklist

For implementation planning, the Implementation Checklist Tool (Figure 8-1C on page 135) will allow you to account for everything you need to get done.

As with any part of your strategy, if you're doing this for the first time, just get done what you can and then move forward. You will learn the most when you put the plan in motion, remember, ***Strategy in Motion***™.

Activity 2: Create Your Scorecards and Action Plans

Starting my career as an engineer with Procter & Gamble, I quickly learned that "you get what you measure" — or at least have a better chance of reaching your targets. I recommend a Strategy Scorecard Tool *and* a Run-the-Business Balanced Scorecard Tool to break down your goals and measure progress. These scorecards are critical to predict and control your current business while adjusting and changing your strategy. The Run-the-Business Scorecard Tool is a communication and tracking tool to manage and forecast your "day-to-day" by focusing on a balanced set of key performance indicators.

The Strategy Scorecard Tool

Below is a Strategy Scorecard Tool — there are a few columns, and it's simpler than it looks:

    1. For each of your three priorities, create no more than three

Strategic Planning Process		
What needs to be done?	**Who will do it?**	**When will it be done?**
Update Strategic Plan Summary	Emily	September 16, 2021
Finalize Strategic Plan Summary	Spencer	October 31, 2021
Finalize Priority Plans -Identify champions and team -Confirm outcomes and initiatives -Determine costs	David Bill Erik	September 16, 2021
Complete short-term Action Plans	TBD by Priority Teams	Refer to Strategic Priority Plans
Finalize Strategic Priority Scorecard	Emily and Strategic Team	After September 16 workshop
Finalize and update Operational Scorecard (KPIs)	Greg, Transition To Dan	Draft by September 16, 2021 Finalize by December 31, 2021
Complete 3- to 5-year Strategic Budget	David	Draft by September 16, 2021
Document a Strategic Communication Plan and include visuals AND organizational communication	Scott and Stefanie	Rollout to organization in October (SOC meetings tentatively scheduled for week of October 11 and October 18)
Link strategic measures to operations/individuals	Emily, Transition to Melinda	September 30, 2021
Schedule Quarterly Reviews	Emily	September 17, 2021
Clarify team structure including Executive Team, Operational Team and Strategic Team (finalize Team Meeting Calendar)	Spencer	September 15, 2021
Monthly		
What needs to be done?	**Who will do it?**	**When will it be done?**
Hold Priority Task Team meetings to review progress	Strategic Priority Team Champions	Monthly beginning in October
Hold Strategic Team meetings to review strategic priorities and discuss external/internal changes	Spencer	Monthly/quarterly beginning in October
Hold Operational Team meetings to review 'Run the Business' key performance indicators	Eric	Weekly/monthly beginning in October
Quarterly		
What needs to be done?	**Who will do it?**	**When will it be done?**
Update Priority Review Documents	Strategic Priority Team Champions	One week after monthly meetings
Update Strategic Scorecard with actual results	Dave	One week before monthly and quarterly meetings
Prepare agenda for Quarterly Review	Emily	One week before quarterly meetings beginning in December
Hold Quarterly Review	Spencer	Starting in January, 2022
Determine Personal and Company Rocks for the next quarter	Spencer, Executive Team	Two weeks after quarterly reviews
Communicate strategic update to organization	Scott	Three weeks after quarterly reviews
Annually		
What needs to be done?	**Who will do it?**	**When will it be done?**
Assess Process	Emily, Executive Team	By June 30 each year
Update 'Listen and Learn' tools (as needed)	Emily / Scott and Strategic Team	By August 15 each year

FIGURE 8-1C
IMPLEMENTATION CHECKLIST TOOL — CLIENT EXAMPLE
To download, visit stretch-sl.com/SIMtools
or follow the QR code in the Preface

SMART goals and give each an owner.

2. Every SMART goal needs at least one outcome measure. These will take time to find the most effective goals and gain alignment.

3. The baseline for a new strategy is the prior year or the past 12 months.

4. Add a goal for the current year (which the measure should reach.)

5. Then, add a roadmap with key milestones across the four quarters of the current year.

6. Finally, capture your actuals quarter by quarter, YTD Actual, and Status (e.g., "On Track," "Fair," or "Not on Track.")

Remember the **Rule of Three**: no more than *three* strategic priorities and *three or fewer* goals and objectives for each. Implementation plans work if they are simple, focused, and fully supported.

On page 137 is the template for a Strategy Scorecard Tool (Figure 8-2) and here is one that was completed by a client:

Increase Market Share in HealthCare, Team Champion: M. G. Team	1 year target			Roadmap - Key milestones				2021 Actual		
SMART Goal	Owner	baseline (2021)	2022 Target	1st Qtr.	2nd Qtr.	3rd Qtr.	4th Qtr.	Actual (YTD)	Overall Status (on-track, fair,	Comments/Updates
Increase Reoccurring Water Management Revenue with the Addition of New Hospital Key Accounts.	Michael G	KHN contract added XXX in reoccuring revenue.	Add a Hospital Network with 3 to 5 Facilities or 3 to 5 Independent Hospitals Totaling $350.00 to $500.00 in	Networks identified. Identify & updating names/responsibilities. Identifying current provider. Updating confidence meter. Working Sales Playbook	Identifying & updating names/responsibilities. Identifying current provide. Updating confidence meter. Working Sales Playbook..	1-3 Hospital Accounts Added. $75,000 in Revenue. Update confidence meter. Bid 1-3 networks. Working Sales Playbook	1 Hospital Network Added or 3 to 5 Hospital Accounts Added. $$350,000 to $500,000 in Revenue. Update confidence meter. Bid 3-10 networks. Work Sales.	0 Revenue & 0 facilities	On Track	KHN-Stronger WT w/OV & SV, (equip/frequncy) Regularly schedule meetings & new meetings w/Design and Construction. Mercy-Meetings with Design & construction. UC Health-Meeting w/Facility & I.P's TSHE-running golf event
Grow Mechanical Contractor Key Accounts (Rieck, AMS, MSD, TP Mechanical).	Amy R	XXX	XXX	xxk. Building relationship w/service side of mechanicals. Working w/ on first year of warranty service new Construction projects. Symposium (April) research OSBA. researched A Safety Tradeshow	xxk Smyposium. Presentation w/MSD Service team. Estimating team cincy & Columbus.Review of all R accounts. Meeting w/DW to discuss escalation process. Work AM Playbook.	xxk Presentation w/AD. Work escalation process for all Mechanicals. Work AM Playbook	xxk Work escalation process. Work AM Playbook	xxx	On Track	Connor Group first WT contract w/equipment in a while outside of disenfection from TP. Engaged in other activity & quotes for additional WT services. MSD Service Manager communicated to team to use SBT for all heating loops. Multiple touches w/MSD lead estimator of new construction bids.
Technologist Training Plan, Team Champion: D.D, Team Members: C.B.	Team Members:									
Implement a Robust Training Program for the Water Technologist.	Doug Dolder	We have Many Training Materials but, Believe we Need a More Cohesive Program	Build a Training Program that includes validation and periodic refresher training. Establish the expectation for the level of the Technologists expertise our	1. Review current new hire program to include content and validation. 2. Implement improvements.	1. Review ongoing training requirements. 2.Implement Improvements. 3.Decide on "model" program for SBT WT training program.	1. Create training model for future and current techs	1. Communicate and implement new training format. 2. Create formal training plans for all WT's in 2023.	25.00%	On Track	The goal for this priority is training program is complete and implemented. Should be listed as percentage complete under actual YTD
Employee Retention Program: Team Champion: Travis Durham Team Members: Steve Elrich, Chris Miller, Charles Dearing, Peter Veley, Lois Elrich, Jesse Lyall										
Implement an Effective Employee Retention Program. Establish Retention Norms for SBT (focus Water Tech and Sales).	Travis Durham	Based on the last 5 years of hiring data. We have hired 35 people. 14 are still here. Of the 21 that have left, there were 11 folks that left for other job opportunity or because they were unhappy. Of those 11, 4 people were "regrettable losses"	To Establish a Measureable retention plan/program and improve Employee Retention. (regrettable loss) #WT with CWT. We will be developing an acceptable target of "time on the job" for each role and then we will track to that.	1. Identify Scope of Work w/ Cost. 2. Review exit interviews and establish any controlable trends. 3. Come up a percentage of current attrition and establish an acceptible attrition rate. 4. Develop an outline for an employee retention program.	1. Create Employee Value Proposition 2. Decide what offerings, training, and programs stop and what needs started. 3.Review Hiring/Onboarding Process	1. Survey against employee value proposition. Add question at end of Survey: is there anything additional you would like considered in our EVP?. 2. Review survey Data 3. Using compiled data Develop a viable Emp Retention program.	1.Review andFine tune and implement Employee Retention Program. 2 Set a quarterly schedule to review any changes that need to be made.	22.20%	On Track	Track as a percentage. Set the baseline of regrettable loss as a percentage based on current data. Create acceptable retention years per role (IE Water tech 5 years). If 5 years is acceptable how do we maximize that roll in those years and where does the CWT fit in (another role?). have a general employee value prop and a specific value prop for roles - IE water tech & sales. what is expected retention for sales?

FIGURE 8-2C
STRATEGY SCORECARD TOOL — CLIENT EXAMPLE

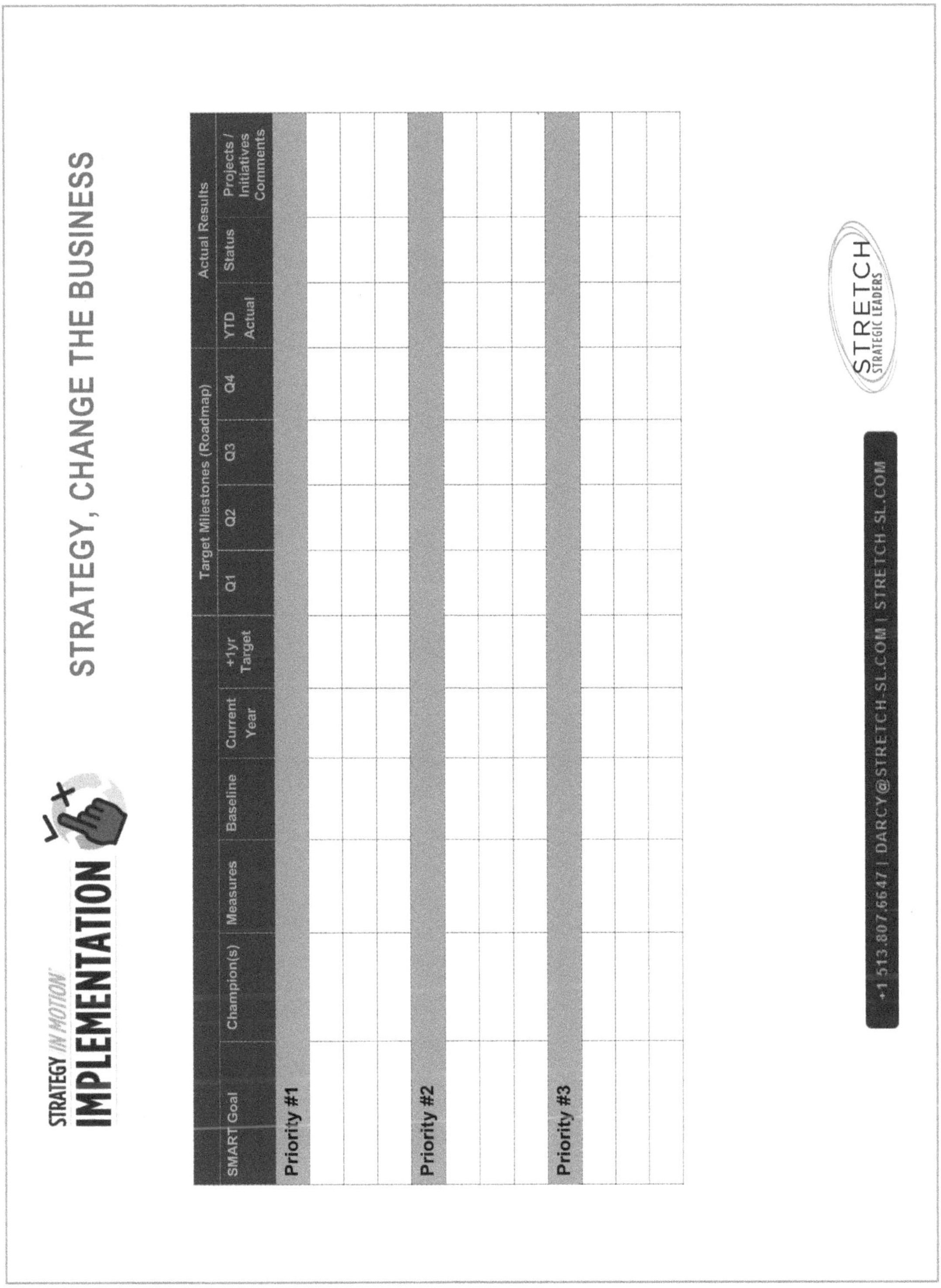

FIGURE 8-2
STRATEGY SCORECARD TOOL
To download, visit stretch-sl.com/SIMtools or follow the QR code in the Preface

A strategic scorecard should be updated *quarterly*.

The Run-the-Business Balanced Scorecard Tool

On page 139 is the template for a "balanced scorecard" (Figure 8-3)—it balances traditional metrics (for example, revenue) with non-financial measures to get an all-round picture of how things are going. The balanced scorecard framework has been around for many years and is a very helpful tool for managing leading and lagging indicators.

Below is a completed scorecard from a client (Figure 8-3C):

Objective	Measures	Owner	Frequency	Monthly Baseline	Monthly Target	Annual Goal	Jan	Feb	March	April	May
Financial											
Revenue	$ MM	DB	M								
Profit	% Gross Margin	DB	M								
Debt Ratio	% of Assets Financed	KG	M								
Current Ratio	Ratio	KG	M								
Customer											
New Clients	# / Revenue?	GE	M								
Satisfaction (Calls to Key Accounts)	Satisfaction Index (NPS)	GE	W								
On-time Delivery	% on-time	WO	W								
Response Time	Minutes/Hours	WO	D								
Pipeline	$Revenue in Sales Funnel	GE	W								
Internal Processes											
Quality	Tests out of Range	WO	D								
Unbillable Service Hours	$ M	KG	W								
Available Technician Hours.	Hours	KG	W								
Accounts Receivable	# A/R DSO	KG	M								
Return Service Calls (Rework)	$ M	WO	W								
Learning/Organizational Development											
Overtime	%	WO	M								
Safety - Lost Time	Days Lost	SS	M								
Safety - Incidents	# of Incidents	SS	M								
Training	Annual Hours	PE	M								
Culture	Core values awared	PE	M								

RTB (Run the Business) Balanced Scorecard - Key Performance Indicators (KPIs)

Red — > 70% vs.Target
Yellow — < 70% vs.Target
White — On Target
Green — Above Target

Owner Responsibilities
1. Utilize Measurement Template(s)
2. Verify Measure/Formula
3. Define Measurement Information
4. Determine Data Elements and Sources
5. Determine approach for tracking measure
6. Define baseline and targets

FIGURE 8-3C
**RUN-THE-BUSINESS BALANCED SCORECARD TOOL —
CLIENT EXAMPLE**

The Run-the-Business Balanced Scorecard Tool is like the Strategy Scorecard Tool, but the targets are tactical, and the results are measured and updated *monthly*.

Each scorecard (Strategy and Run-the-Business) needs its own leader and team, ideally with different people on each. This is key to building capacity.

Action Plans

This is a good time to start preparing the action plans for key project/initiatives in your priority plans. Some clients utilize action plans better than others. It is really up to your company on how much de-

OPERATIONS, RUN THE BUSINESS

STRATEGY *IN MOTION*
IMPLEMENTATION

Balanced Scorecard							Monthly				Actual Results		
Objective	Champion(s)	Measures	Baseline	Monthly Target	+1yr Target	Jan	Feb	March	April	YTD Actual	% of Actual	Status / Comment
Financial												
Customer / Market												
Internal Processes												
People/Learning/Organizational Development												

STRETCH
STRATEGIC LEADERS

+1 513.807.6647 | DARCY@STRETCH-SL.COM | STRETCH-SL.COM

FIGURE 8-3
RUN-THE-BUSINESS BALANCED SCORECARD TOOL
To download, visit stretch-sl.com/SIMtools or follow the QR code in the Preface

tail is needed. The more complicated and involved the key initiative/ project is, the more important it is to have a clear action plan. The Priority Action Plan Tool (Figure 8-4) is on page 141.

Activity 3: Optimize Your Leadership Teams

Now that your plan is completed, it is time to develop the supporting systems to implement and execute. Cyndi Wineinger, a team dynamic expert, believes each team needs a leader, clear purpose, and roles. Structurally, we recommend three key teams: the executive team, the strategic team, and the operational (Run-the-Business) team. You will want to adjust your teams to fit the tiers and responsibilities based on roles and responsibilities, see Figure 8-5:

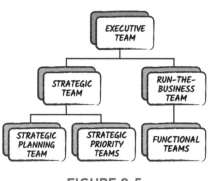

FIGURE 8-5
TEAM OPTIMIZATION

When I start the strategic planning process with a company, leaders often wear many hats and are in too many meetings. We call this the "leadership stew," and Pat Lencioni has some great books on this (*The Five Dysfunctions of a Team*[2] is one of my favorites).

At this point I remind my clients, "No-one has time for another meeting, until they are not included." I developed this quote after years of working with key leaders in too many meetings who don't trust the process if they are not there.

My experience has proven that we must build trust and separate "strategic" conversations from "run-the-business" conversations. The right-hand side is straightforward: the team runs the day-to-day business and manages goals and metrics daily, weekly, and monthly. It's critical to build capacity in this team, so executives have more time to focus on long-term planning.

The left-hand side will probably be new to you: we have an overall strategic team split into two functions, (1) Planning (the strategic planning team) and (2) Priority execution (namely, the implementation teams for the three priorities). Planning is usually done every year, and Priorities, once the strategic plan is complete, are how the team implements the plan and meets at least monthly, sometimes weekly.

Companies should define the teams, identify the champions (leaders of the team), and clarify the structure to build the rhythm. Building a

2 Lencioni, Patrick. *The Five Dysfunctions of a Team*. Jossey-Bass, 2002.

ACTION/PROJECT PLAN

Priority:	
Key /Initiative/Project:		Owner:	
Date:		Revision:	
Standards of Performance *(key measures with target)*:	

Step #	Step	Start Date	End Date	Who	Who Else	Status/Comments

Total Duration of Action Plan: **Latest Acceptable Completion Date:**

Resources Needed (people, money, equipment, etc.):

Overall Comments:

+1 513.807.6647 | DARCY@STRETCH-SL.COM | STRETCH-SL.COM

STRETCH
STRATEGIC LEADERS

FIGURE 8-4
PRIORITY ACTION PLAN TOOL
To download, visit stretch-sl.com/SIMtools or follow the QR code in the Preface

meeting calendar will channel conversation with the right people in the room, and meetings become much more effective. There is an example of this on page 143 (Figure 8-6).

The scorecards, action plans, and the team meeting schedule form the framework for the first three **Implementation** steps.

The final and most challenging step is communicating your strategy and its execution to your organization.

Activity 4: Plan Who Will Communicate the Strategy and How

Strategy is a science, but communication is an art. People can't read your mind; for folks to help, they need to know *how* they can help and — even more importantly — *why* you need help. Many books, blogs, and articles cover effective communication because it's a common business challenge. When I conduct strategic employee surveys for clients, communication is *always* one of their top three improvement areas.

There are many communication vehicles — company meetings, stories, town halls, one-on-one meetings, leadership meetings, team meetings, emails, website, internet, visual management, dashboards, employee manuals, customer and employee newsletters — the list is endless.

Your job is to figure out what works best for your company and use multiple approaches. Most people are visual learners — so guess what happens during meetings if you're only talking and there is nothing visual? You'll sound like Charlie Brown's teacher: "Wah, wah, wah, wah."

Which Communication Channels Should You Use?

Here is a valuable reference that illustrates how people retain information.

A lecture: Information retention is 5%
Reading: Information retention is 10%
Audio-visual: Information retention is 20%
Demonstration: Information retention is 30%
Discussion group: Information retention is 50%
Practice by doing: Information retention is 75%
Teaching others: Information retention is 90%

Did you get all that? If you closed your eyes, can you recall any communication channel and its corresponding retention percentage? You were reading, so typically, you would remember one or two.

People assimilate information in a myriad of ways, but using visuals is almost always better than talking or reading. On page 144, there is a graph that shows you the same data visually.

STRATEGY *IN MOTION*
IMPLEMENTATION

High Performing Teams Calendar

Team	Leader	Attendees (Roles)	Frequency	Time/Day	Location	Primary Objective	Reports Provided
Executive Team	President/CEO	Key Executives	Weekly	1 hour	TBD	Review KPIs – key performance indicators Operational Issues Strategic Issues Resource Allocation	KPIs
Operational – Run the Business Review	COO / VP Operations	Run the Business Team (Key Department heads)	Weekly monthly	1 hour 2-3 hours	TBD	Manage KPIs Cross department communication – Department updates State of the business Operational Issues Strategic update	Run the Business Scorecard Follow-ups / Corrective Actions
Strategic - Change the Business Review	Strategic Process Owner	Strategic team	Monthly Quarterly	2-4 hour 4-8 hours	Conf room	External "Look up" Internal changes Assess strategic directions Address strategic issues	Priority reviews Strategy scorecard Updated action plans Rocks
Priority reviews	Strategic Priority Champions	Strategic Priority teams	At least monthly	4-6 hours a month	TBD	Keep Activities on track Manage challenges/barriers	Strategic Priority Plans Action Plans
Board of Advisors	President / CEO	3-5 Outside Advisors	Quarterly	4-6 hours a quarterly	TBD	External "Look up" Internal changes Assess strategic directions Discuss strategic issues Open Forum	Board book / info 1 week prior to meeting

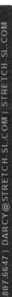

STRETCH
STRATEGIC LEADERS

+1 513 .807 .6647 | DARCY@STRETCH-SL.COM | STRETCH-SL.COM

FIGURE 8-6
TEAM MEETING CALENDAR TOOL
To download, visit stretch-sl.com/SIMtools or follow the QR code in the Preface

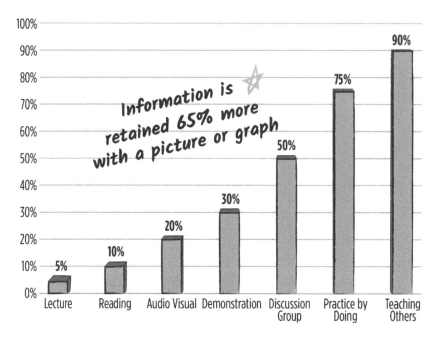

FIGURE 8-7
HOW INFORMATION IS RETAINED

Hopefully, the graph was a better medium than the list was! Indeed, you should consider even more effective vehicles and channels for communications with your team.

Communication plans should include different channels (all-company meetings, emails, one-on-one meetings, websites, videos, training manuals, etc.) to reinforce the message and increase information retention. It's also good to remember that not all people learn in the same way, so it's best to implement a variety of communication modes. **This is a great place for a marketing or communication resource to help you!**

What Should You Do First?

The leadership must *know* and *be able to repeat* the six core strategic concepts: core purpose, core values, vision, business definition/core focus, differentiator, and strategic priorities.

When I finish a strategic planning process, the most crucial group to communicate these questions to is the executive team — they need to understand and support the six answers, modeling by example. So, the next couple of meetings involve a "pop quiz" with the leadership team (Figure 8-8 on page 145). By the way, I tell them we will continue to have the pop quiz until everyone gets 100%, so is that really a pop quiz?

STRATEGY *IN MOTION*
PLAN DEVELOPMENT

6 Core Strategic
Questions

Company Purpose	(The Why – why you do what you do)
Co. Core Values	The How – essential characteristics that define success in your organization)
Vision	(Desired State - where do you see the organization to be in 5-10 years)
Business Definition / Core Focus	(What specifically does your company do and for whom, consider your where you should win)
Strategic Advantage	(Your Strategic Differentiator(s), what makes you unique/different, What is your Measurable Brand Promise)
1-2 year Strategic Priorities (make or breaks to address strategic issues and achieve the vision)	**Strategic Priorities**

+1 513.807.6647 | DARCY@STRETCH-SL.COM | STRETCH-SL.COM

STRETCH
STRATEGIC LEADERS

FIGURE 8-8
6 CORE STRATEGIC QUESTIONS TOOL
To download, visit stretch-sl.com/SIMtools or follow the QR code in the Preface

145

Some team members find pop quizzes too stressful! Seriously, maybe this is why the owner freezes. However, this is critical because it forces us to align with our answers so that we can then recall and share them with employees (without looking at the wall).

When the leadership team nails the core strategic questions, which might take a couple of monthly meetings, they can begin sharing the strategy with groups of employees. As I have mentioned, please don't put these six statements on a T-shirt right away, but do start having conversations about them. In my experience, companies that are new to strategic planning are still adjusting these for a while. It allows your employees to discuss, practice, and teach others.

Like we saw with Figure 8-7!

What Do Our People Want to Know?

Once you have a good grasp of your core strategic questions, it is time to start telling everyone about them over and over (and over) again. **It takes a while for people to hear new information and even longer to believe it.** In my opinion, everyone (yes, everyone!) should know these six core strategic concepts for your company. When I was an Ohio Award for Excellence examiner (AKA state-level Malcolm Baldridge Award), we would walk around the companies and ask... *What are your company's core values? What is your company's vision?*

CASE STUDY

Third-Party Healthcare Administration Company

We finished the first draft of the strategic plan with another of my favorite clients, a third-party administrator for healthcare. The leadership team worked hard and did a fantastic job managing the team, the entire organization, and the customers to define the core strategic questions.

It was time to develop the communication plan, and one of the first documents was a strategic infographic using pictures and text to connect people to the strategy. We involved a group of employees to create the infographic using information from the plan. The infographic was supposed to show the relationship between the purpose, values, core focus, brand promise, and vision.

The first phase was to challenge the concepts and "words." It was a surprising exercise because the employee voice was added to the core strategic questions. This resulted in significant learning; the leadership team took it in stride and listened to their feedback — they made effective changes, and it was now time for the team to create the picture!

Well, meeting after meeting after meeting, the team would show us their work, and it still was just words on a piece of paper with the current branding, which happened to be a kite and a tree. The task team leader was struggling with the infographic tool, and the team was moving so slowly I nearly lost my mind. We kept reminding them to use pictures/graphs/icons to represent the words. I showed them examples and encouraged them to find the examples!

After a couple of months (yep, months), we realized we did not have the right skill set on the team. We had people who thought they understood marketing but had no clue — we needed a true marketing expert! We found the perfect person and added them to the team. Within a month, the team had a draft of the infographic below:

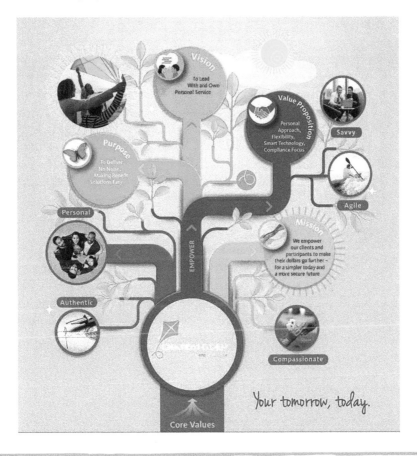

The lesson I learned (and continue to learn, repeatedly) is, "When it comes to communication, you have to slow down in order to go fast." It made complete sense for this team; they were moving slowly, but with each review and working session, the task team became more aware of the core strategic questions and, in the end, all of them could recite them! Success!

Expect Challenges

Michael Porter puts it best in "Michael Porter's Big Ideas": Companies need to remain flexible, moving in a clear direction, yet ready to change! [3]You need to permit challenges to your approaches. Allow active discussions with people in your organization. There is no single measure or scorecard that will tell you where the pitfalls lie in your business strategy.

Check out our website for lots of great options!

Those conversations should be happening with vigor in your executive, strategic, and operational team meetings. **It is also helpful to invest in communication and high-performance team training.** A podcast "How to Avoid Death by Meeting" will help you.[4]

Here are some reasons that meetings have gotten a bad rap: no real purpose, no agenda, too many people, not the right people, dysfunctional people, unprepared people, endless discussions, constant repetition, repeated distractions, no decisions — you get the picture. This does NOT mean you should stop having meetings. Although this would be the easy way out!

Pat Lencioni[5] encourages companies to separate running the business every day from strategy — *ta da!* It's always good to have your approach validated. **My most successful clients have three critical teams with well-planned meetings:**

1. A **weekly executive team** meeting (with strategy as part of the agenda)
2. A **monthly run-the-business/operational** meeting
3. A **monthly strategic team** meeting to review progress on strategic priorities

It's important to fold in more people, and effective meetings are the channel to do this. Be flexible and adaptable — ***Implementation*** is not a straight line to your goals, so you need all the help you can get to find the way!

---

3   Hammonds, Keith H. "Michael Porter's Big Ideas." *Fast Company*, 2 Feb. 2001. https://www.fastcompany.com/42485/michael-porters-big-ideas
4   Quattrochi, Mark, host. "How To Avoid Death by Meeting!" *X with Q*, 63, Simplecast, 3 January 2022, https://x-with-q.simplecast.com/episodes/how-to-avoid-death-by-meeting-XVNiUcOo
5   Lencioni, Patrick. *Death by Meeting — A Leadership Fable*. Jossey Bass, 2004.

Communicate, Communicate, and Communicate

Your job as a leader is to deliver the strategic direction and priorities constantly and consistently. Unfortunately, when half of the middle-managers can't name any of their company's strategic priorities, this is not engagement! People need to hear and experience new information repeatedly before they remember it. We discussed earlier in this chapter how information is retained, and we learned that **"teaching others" clocks 90-95% for retention**, so offering your leadership team and employees opportunities to instruct others in the six core strategic questions will increase their retention. The entire leadership team should be responsible for communicating strategy, not just the president or owner.

Remember to use pictures and infographics. Watch "Draw your Future" which reminds us of the power of images.[6] **How much do we remember from a picture? At least 65% more.** Images are emotional and our brain reacts more quickly to images, validating the expression "a picture is worth a thousand words."

Moving Forward

I tell my clients to think about "doubling the strategic capacity" each time we develop and update the strategy; **we need to involve 100% more people.** So, if you have five people on the strategic planning team, find five additional key leaders to engage in the implementation. The best place to involve them is the "strategic priorities" part.

Think about this: if the first time you do strategic planning, you involve five key leaders, then during the rollout, you involve five more people, now you have 10. For the next update, your goal is to involve 10 more, then 20. For larger companies, you will push strategy down to business units, markets, and teams, keeping your whole company connected.

As with anything new, it takes a couple of iterations to get it right, with a complete strategic plan in place. **We will implement the best plan we can during the first year, improving with practice.**

As you complete *Phase 3: Implementation*, you will have:
- A strategy scorecard.
- A run-the-business scorecard.
- A team meetings schedule and plan.
- An organizational (team optimization) chart for leadership teams.
- A communications plan, including the six answers to the core strategic questions, the communications tactics you will use, and how you will share the strategy across the company.

6   "Draw Your Future." *YouTube*, uploaded by ThisIsRealBusiness, 4 Jan. 2013, https://www.youtube.com/watch?v=A7KRSCyLqc4.

On to the final ***Strategy in Motion***™ phase — ***Strategic Management***.

Chapter Summary

In this chapter, you:
- Built a strategy scorecard to track progress on your strategic priority goals.
- Built a run-the-business scorecard to manage the day-to-day goals and KPIs of the business.
- Created a leadership team structure focusing on both strategy and routine business.
- Assembled a meeting schedule and cadence for all the leadership teams.
- Gathered the answers to the six core strategic questions.
- Planned your communications rollout, including all of the executive team — not just the president.

NOTES

NOTES

STRATEGY
IN MOTION ™

PHASE 4: Strategic Management

CHAPTER 9

Strategic Management

> *"Flexibility and adaptability are key.*
> *Remember, it gets easier with practice."*
> **—Darcy Bien**

Why Do You Need Strategic Management?

Companies who successfully implement their strategy are 12% more profitable, and 70% of companies with a plan outperform their competition. However, most companies fail at execution — remember it's hard work to change, but it's worth it!

The big question is, do you have the *people* and *structures* you need to implement your strategy? In our remote, post-pandemic, high-tech world, there are many opportunities and a whole host of threats. Getting your people engaged in your strategy execution is your highest priority, so we will first look at "who" and then "what." The "who" is definitely the most challenging part.

In This Chapter

PHASE 4 STRATEGIC MANAGEMENT

>> **"Look Up"**
Monthly

Assess
>> Quarterly

Update
>> Annually

>> **Invest** in
Training

In this chapter, we're navigating how to manage your strategic plan execution through the rough waters of business reality.

During **Phase 4: Strategic Management**, you'll create your support structure for the next 12-18 months.

The key strategic questions you're trying to answer are:

1. Do we have the right people for our planned future?
2. How will we manage our strategy to ensure successful outcomes?

Start with "Who"

Organizations, especially smaller ones, have "non-performers" in essential roles. Sometimes, they're family — that's a whole other story — but they are often loyal employees and charming people who lack the capabilities you need moving forward. They got you to where you are today, but they don't have the skills to get you to tomorrow. **To grow a company successfully (and not get stuck), you need different skill sets, strong performers, and people who invest in good relationships.** Without the right people, skill sets, and a commitment to high performing teams, you will get stuck and, unfortunately, frustrated.

CASE STUDY

Episode 1

One of my most epic fails from years ago was utterly predictable. I loved the founder and had a great relationship with one of his key leaders, who was wholly committed to strategic planning.

I often start with Patrick Lencioni's team development model and use the *Five Dysfunctions of a Team*[1] assessment.

These were the results for my client.

When I saw it, I was worried — my gut told me to stop the project immediately. However, the leaders agreed to work through it, and I believed them, so we proceeded with strategic planning. I know how to get a plan done and have NEVER gotten stuck in the planning process.

There were major trust issues with the wrong people in the wrong seats and an aversion to transparency, but the crazy outcome was that we *did* push through and developed a good draft of the strategic plan. We identified the top three strategic priorities; one was "increase trust and teamwork" — no kidding!

---

1   Lencioni, Patrick. *Five Dysfunctions of a Team*. Jossey Bass, 2002. The Assessment is a helpful and inexpensive way to measure your teamwork. You'll find it at thetablegroup.com.

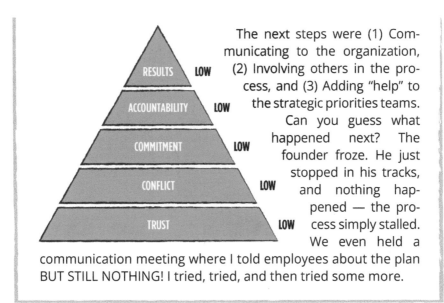

The next steps were (1) Communicating to the organization, (2) Involving others in the process, and (3) Adding "help" to the strategic priorities teams. Can you guess what happened next? The founder froze. He just stopped in his tracks, and nothing happened — the process simply stalled. We even held a communication meeting where I told employees about the plan BUT STILL NOTHING! I tried, tried, and then tried some more.

I still feel guilty about not stopping the process after the team assessment, which clearly showed a very dysfunctional team. Most strategic planners are great process people but NOT so strong at working through the "people" issues; what was missing was an organizational development expert. As I have mentioned many times, I am focused on the process, working with your strategic teams and pushing them to move forward. This is a great example of a company who needed an organizational expert to build their self-awareness and capacity to trust, and then focus on strategic planning.

Like most people, you're probably stronger in *either* process or people — which is your strength? The client needed an expert to help with trust problems, and it starts with a behavior assessment which is its own expertise.

Episode 2

CASE STUDY

Fast forward. I partnered with Cyndi Wineinger, my "all things people" partner, an expert who helps with organizational development. The leader from my failed client decided to revisit strategic planning, focusing only on his business unit. Cyndi led with Birkman® Assessments, one-on-one coaching, team dynamics, and communication training,[2] while I led the strategic planning development.

---

2 "The Birkman Method." *Birkman*, https://birkman.com/the-birkman-method/.

Recently, the client texted me and said, "Thank you, Darcy, for pushing me through the strategic planning process! I don't know what I would be doing with my company right now if we hadn't done it. We are now positioned very well to come through this downturn with a company that will survive and has strong growth."

Here's the timing — we completed his integrated strategy and people process in 2019 (before the pandemic). The text was dated April 2020 (during the pandemic). Today, he is well-positioned with a formidable team and has made it through.

The Right People?

Here are two questions I ask my clients when they are struggling with a people decision:

1. *Would you hire them again?* If your answer is no, then find then a coach or a replacement.
2. *If they gave you their resignation, how would you feel?* Relieved? Guess what? You may be part of the problem! You haven't committed to getting the right people in every seat.

The most difficult decision I have seen owners wrestle with is letting go of a loyal employee. This is a tough decision, and, in my experience, an outside, highly qualified resource can help!

It is all about the people. If you are unsure about the people on your leadership team and they are not willing to make changes, the strategic plan will suffer — maybe not in the first year, but most likely during the second or third year. The key is to realize early if you need to change or add people — allow yourself time to plan the change and carry it through.

The goal is "great" people who trust each other. How great they are and how much they trust will have a huge impact on your company's ability to develop and implement a strategic plan — which is the difference between "winning" and "not-winning" (AKA failing).

How Do You Know Who is "Missing" From Your Team?

You may have a question: "How do I know who might be lacking from my team?" It's one thing to fit the jigsaw pieces of your teams together, but it's another to realize that some pieces might be missing.

Nearly every executive team needs critical functions to be present: finance, operations, marketing, sales, HR, IT, and the top people — owner/CEO/President. In the early days, your executives (and employees) may have been wearing multiple hats, for example, one executive managing marketing and sales. As the company grows, the weight of the work expands, and jobs need to be split. Functions that seemed less critical become important and need focus.

Organizational development is a whole different discipline, and I will touch on this topic in the final chapter with an example of how certain functions become more critical to support a strategy and its implementation.

The High-Performance Culture

Strategic planning involves change, so we need a culture willing to change: a high-performance culture. The only other culture is one focused on low performance; it's that simple! We all know the leader of Dilbert's company is not that smart, and, as a result, his team has lots of material to share![3]

I can tell by the first meeting with the leadership team whether the strategy has a chance or not. Is the owner at the meeting? Does the meeting start on time? Do people speak up? Is there healthy conflict? Is their strategy the same as the previous year?

Like it or not, the ability to "win" truly starts with leadership as the role models. Deep down you know how much employees look at people in leadership positions and "assume" the behaviors. If a leader is not a mirror of the core values, then employees *assume* it's ok to behave as leaders do, or even that being contrary to core values is how you get to "win around here." Imagine you have a sales manager with a rather big ego — and I'm not saying sales managers all have big egos, but maybe this one does. Think Herb Tarlek on *WKRP in Cincinnati*. This sales manager treats people disrespectfully and doesn't follow established protocols or processes. I don't want to sound like a Debbie Downer, but every experience an employee has with this person reinforces this negative behavior as permissible and negatively impacts your culture.

You know what they say about assuming...

If you don't have the right people, you're wasting your investment and annoying your good people, who can't understand why you're not acting. All successful teams start with good, solid people committed to common goals; think of your people as an investment rather than a cost. Get some help and make some changes.

Good people =
Good investment

Then "What"

Building the foundation of a successful implementation with a strong strategic plan. A good plan should:

- **Determine what makes you different**
  - Your unique activities
  - What do you do better than anyone?
- **Focus on what you do best with the "right" people**
  - People who represent core values
  - People with passion
  - Right people, right positions
- **"Change" your business**
  - Competitive advantage over the long-term
  - Sustainable (hard to replicate)
- **Address critical performance issues**
  - Operational excellence is a given
  - "Front line leaders" should be focused on running the business
- **Create the right balance**
  - Change management is critical
- **Be both Visionary and Flexible**
  - Conveys desired state and allows adjustments
- **Guide decision-making at all levels**
  - Linked to the organization

Manage the strategic process to ensure confidence and learning:

- This is only the beginning — remember, it gets easier with practice.
- Strategic execution depends on leadership. Team involvement and development are critical.
- Strategy can only improve the odds of success.
- Implementation of any strategic plan is dependent on commitment and willingness to change.
- Assignments from strategic planning must be treated as essential.
- Flexibility and adaptability are key, AND the teams must watch the goals.

Structure Follows Strategy

Once you have a solid team and a good strategic plan, commit to change to support growth. "Invest in structure to support growth" becomes one of the strategic priorities for many of my clients and is part of the process. It takes time, resources, and in most cases, outside support to change your current structure of people, processes, and systems so you can reach the next level of growth.

The Phases/Who Does What?

In **Strategic Management**, you will learn how to manage your strategic implementation over the timeframe you set (usually 12-18 months). You will:
  • Get ready for launch.
  • Design your monitoring and support plan.

The Activities Overview

Here's the map for team activity in **Phase 4: Strategic Management**:

> **Activity 1: Strategic Process Owner and Their Training**. Invest in your Strategic Process Owner and consider additional training and the Internal Strategic Planner Certification.
> **Activity 2: Plan Your Review Process**. Plan monthly, quarterly, and annual reviews and define charters and tools.
> **Activity 3: The Strategic Process Checklist Tool**. Complete your Strategic Project Checklist.

> *Initiated by the Strategic planning team leader. Completed by the Strategic planning team, including Owners.* **In addition:** *During* **Strategic Management**, *you will need help from HR, finance, marketing, and departmental heads.*

Activity 1: Strategic Process Owner and Their Training

The Strategic Process Owner needs your support and relevant training to execute your plan. By relevant training, I mean a working knowledge of the process of strategic planning and the methods and tools used to support the creation and execution of a strategic plan. I consider this person the on-going internal strategic planning champion. They keep the process working and improving.

Now strategic planning has numerous variants and flavors. The checklist on page 162 is built around my **Strategy in Motion**™ **Process** (see Appendix 2 for more details):

STRATEGY *IN MOTION* ·
STRATEGIC MANAGEMENT

Internal Strategic Planner
Certification Checklist

COMPANY: STRATEGIC PLANNER: DATE:	Completion Date	Comments	Sign-off
Books: *Simplified Strategic Planning* (Bradford and Duncan) *Team-Based Strategic Planning* (Fogg) *Beyond Entrepreneurship* (Collins and Lazier) - optional			
Listen and Learn (Data-Gathering)			
Articles: "My Printer Broke" (Darcy Bien) "The Playbook by True Strategic Leaders" (Cyndi Wineinger and Darcy Bien) "Feedback is a Gift" (Darcy Bien) "Importance of Stakeholder Goals" (Darcy Bien) "How to Conduct Research" (Jane Meyer)			
Understand video, "What is Strategy"			
Discuss the importance of the Strategic Planning "Process"			
Complete Strategic Planning Assessment / Audit tool			
Certification on Strategic Team Charter tool			
Complete Stakeholder Goals tool			
Certification of Current Momentum/Financial Analysis tool			
Certification of Strategic Survey tool (planning team, employees)			
Certification of Customer Survey tool			
Certification on Competitor Analysis tool			
Certification of Business Segmentation tool			
Certification of Market Segment Analysis			
Certification on Industry 7 factors tool			
Certification of SWOT tool			

+1 513.807.6647 | DARCY@STRETCH-SL.COM | STRETCH-SL.COM

STRETCH
STRATEGIC LEADERS

FIGURE 9-1
INTERNAL STRATEGIC PLANNER: CERTIFICATION CHECKLIST
To download, visit stretch-sl.com/SIMtools or follow the QR code in the Preface

It is also beneficial to have a clear understanding of the responsibilities of team members. I have customized a Strategic Team Charter for many clients, including Figure 9-2 on page 164.

Activity 2: Plan Your Review Process

I included a team and meeting structure to support your implementation in the previous chapter. How do you use them as you go forward?

Monitoring

You need a monitoring process across all teams that activates monthly, quarterly, and annually. Here are the activities I recommend:

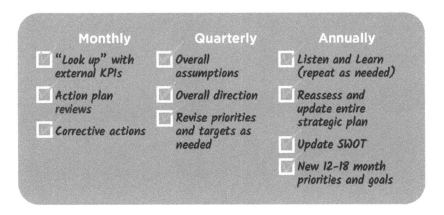

Monthly	Quarterly	Annually
☑ "Look up" with external KPIs	☑ Overall assumptions	☑ Listen and Learn (repeat as needed)
☑ Action plan reviews	☑ Overall direction	☑ Reassess and update entire strategic plan
☑ Corrective actions	☑ Revise priorities and targets as needed	☑ Update SWOT
		☑ New 12–18 month priorities and goals

FIGURE 9-3
STRATEGIC MANAGEMENT MONITORING PROCESS

The cadence shown above is for monitoring; the strategy team and priority teams should meet with the Strategic Process Owner to review the items above. Monthly and quarterly meetings ensure goals for each team are met and to course correct as needed. The annual meeting revisits the overall strategic plan and sets goals and priorities for the following year.

As you can see, this is a cyclical process that incorporates a feedback loop for everyone involved. Assuming you have the right team, this process will ensure your vision and goals are fulfilled.

The Monthly and Quarterly Meetings

The cadence of meetings and monitoring is now clear. Both the strategic team and the priority teams meet separately for the monthly

STRATEGY
TEAM CHARTER

Team Name:	Strategic Planning Team
Purpose:	• Develop and implement our strategic plan. • To provide feedback and recommendations on strategic direction. • To support the long-term stakeholder goals.
Timeframe:	2020/2021
Team Sponsor:	Executive Leadership Team
Team Leader:	TBD
Team Members:	Executive Team and Key Strategic Leaders
Team Resources:	Darcy Bien, Strategy Consultant
Team Member Duties:	1. Active participation in strategic planning sessions, monthly and quarterly update meetings (as needed) 2. Develop external channels/resources to stay updated on key external information/changes and communicate back to the group. 3. Review the Strategic Scorecard and discuss corrective actions. 4. Participate in the setting and implementation of strategic initiatives for strategic priorities. 5. Ensure key strategic initiatives are on track. 6. Support, communicate and promote our strategies throughout the office.
Success Measures:	1. Strategic Scorecard is updated and results are tracked. >80% on-track 2. Key initiatives are on track, or adjustments are made to ensure success. 3. Strategic communication improves. Monthly update, Quarterly 4. Inter-office and department teamwork is increased.
Boundaries:	1. The strategic focus areas must be aligned with our purpose, core values, and vision. 2. Projects and initiatives must be in support of the strategic plan.
Operating Guidelines:	1. The team will meet monthly for 2-4 hours and quarterly for 4-8 hours. 2. Meeting summary and follow-ups will be sent by the Team leader/Note taker. 3. Team members are prepared for the meetings. 4. Team members complete individual assignments on time.
Standing Agenda:	• External Look-up / Indicators. • Review and discuss Scorecard results. Gap analysis of outcomes not on target. • Discuss new external information/changes and new strategic issues. • Priority update/corrective actions. • Follow-ups from prior meeting.

+1 513.807.6647 | Darcy@stretch-sl.com | stretch-sl.com

FIGURE 9-2
STRETCH CHARTER FOR STRATEGIC TEAM
To download, visit stretch-sl.com/SIMtools or follow the QR code in the Preface

meetings. Ideally, the priority teams meet first and feed results, including their scorecard(s) and their action plan updates for the strategic priorities.

Your Strategic Process Owner is tasked with ensuring all documents are ready for the strategic team to review.

The quarterly job of the strategic team is to function as the buffer between the strategic plan and the original intent of the owner and executive team. This is the opportunity to assess progress on each of the strategic priority teams and their action plans, activities, and results. If you have a board, the quarterly strategic review should also be on the agenda for the meeting.

Typically, the strategic team is looking at assumptions to check if they are still valid, updating any new information on the SWOT grid, and completing a summary of the status of priorities.

A tool that supports this is the Quarterly Priority Review Tool (Figure 9-4 on page 166) which the strategic team should complete from updates provided by the priority teams.

Finally, the Strategy Scorecard Tool needs to be updated and color coded by status ("on track," "fair," "not on track") with new quarterly information:

Walk the Walk		1 year target			Roadmap				2020 Actual		
SMART Goals	Owner	2019	2020	2021	Q3	Q4	Q1	Q2	Actual (YTD)	Overall Status (on-track, fair, not-on-track)	Comments/ Updates
Establish an Engagement Survey Baseline	Pam / Cindy	NA	Survey in place by EOY	Improve	Task Team, Research	Determine Survey	Conduct Survey	Action Plan to improve	2/3 research complete	on target	meet with 2 providers, developing
Roll-out strategy with communication and training materials	Andy / Jim / Matt	NA	2 company-wide meetings, 1 page Strategic Infographic	4 company wide meetings	Task Team, Company Meeting	Company Meeting	Company Meeting, Visuals	Company Meeting, update orientations, training, hiring	Marketing Support	Not on Track	Focused on internal strategic communication first, need to move forward
Update and Alignment Organization chart with Role Clarity	Andy / Pam		Role Description updated for Leadership team	Team Structure	draft Role Descriptions	Finalize role descriptions	Team Structure implemented	Succession planning	Birkman training	on target	draft role descriptions complete, need to finalize

FIGURE 9-5C
STRATEGY SCORECARD TOOL — CLIENT EXAMPLE

Annual Review

The annual review is an opportunity to assess the work for the current year and create the plan for the next.

Both the strategic team and the priority teams need to follow the quarterly processes. In addition, the strategic planning team goes through phases 1-4 of the **Strategy in Motion**™ **Process** (deciding where to focus), updates the strategic plan if needed and plans for the following year.

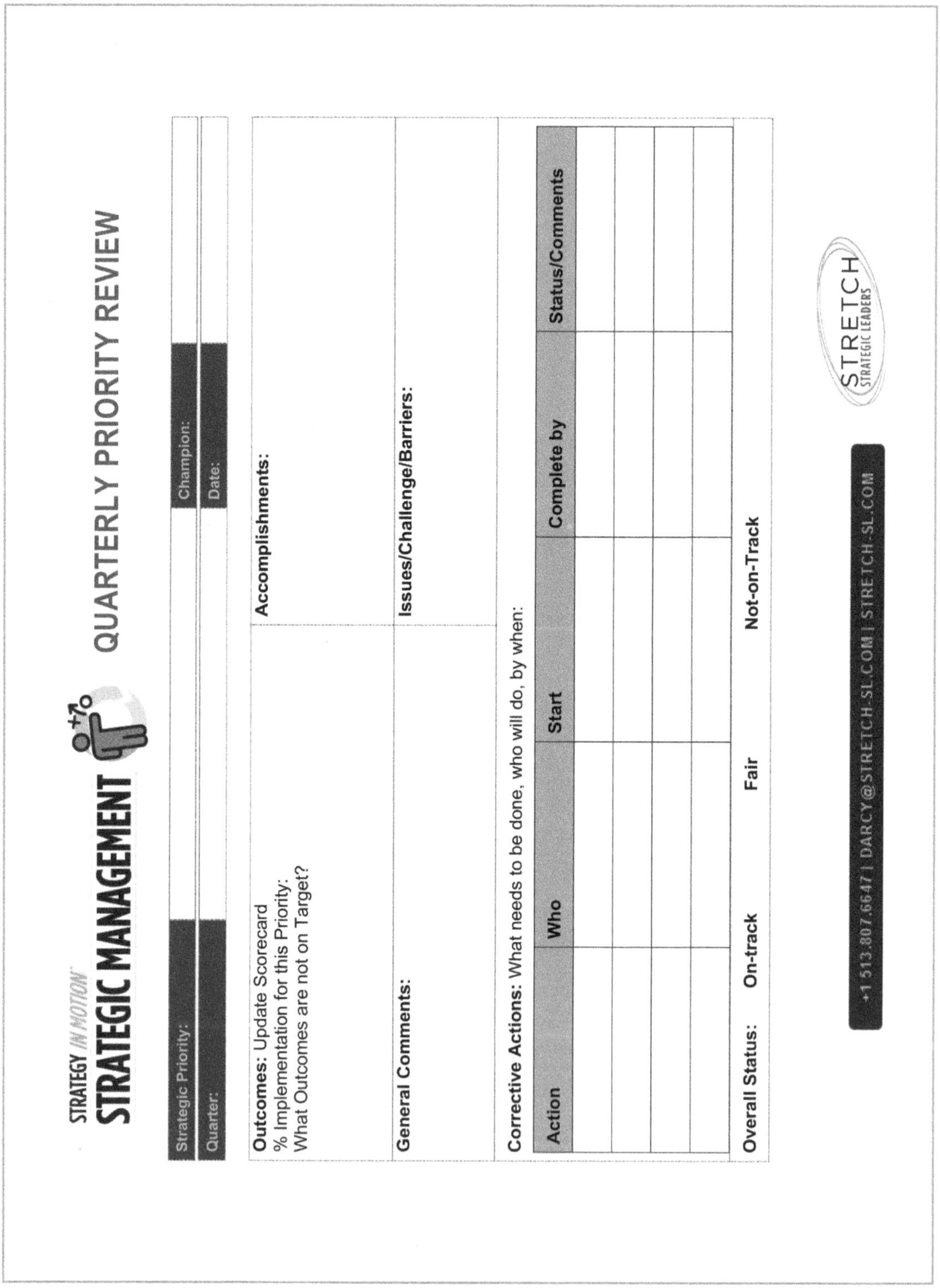

STRATEGY IN MOTION

STRATEGIC MANAGEMENT

QUARTERLY PRIORITY REVIEW

Strategic Priority:

Quarter:

Champion:

Date:

Outcomes: Update Scorecard
% Implementation for this Priority:
What Outcomes are not on Target?

Accomplishments:

General Comments:

Issues/Challenge/Barriers:

Corrective Actions: What needs to be done, who will do, by when:

Action	Who	Start	Complete by	Status/Comments

Overall Status: On-track   Fair   Not-on-Track

STRETCH
STRATEGIC LEADERS

+1 513.807.6647 | DARCY@STRETCH-SL.COM | STRETCH-SL.COM

FIGURE 9-4
QUARTERLY PRIORITY REVIEW TOOL
To download, visit stretch-sl.com/SIMtools or follow the QR code in the Preface

Typically, the strategic planning team:
- Repeats **Listen and Learn** components (e.g., customer surveys).
- Reassesses the **strategic plan** and completes updates.
- Updates the **SWOT** (e.g., opportunities may have become strengths, weaknesses may have been resolved).
- Sets the **priorities and goals** (and measures) for the next 12-18 months.

Choose Your Tools

In choosing your tools, you're looking for solutions to improve collaboration and communication between the teams. These tools will be electronic and provide features and functions to help with project management and offer a document storage option.

You may already have a robust tool in place. That's great. There are many possible solutions, *and* the biggest challenge is having your teams *use them*!

If you need better capabilities to hold everything together, consider tools like Basecamp, Asana, Monday, SmartSheets, and/or MS Power BI.

Activity 3: The Strategic Planning Checklist Tool

Your final step in **Strategic Management** is to complete the Strategic Process Checklist Tool (Figure 9-6 on page 168) for the whole **Strategy in Motion™ Process**. This ensures you didn't miss anything vital, and you'll be ready for the annual review in a year.

Although you may have skipped activities the first time, that's okay. Remember — it's not about perfection!

As you complete **Strategy in Motion™ Phase 4: Strategic Management**, you will have:
- A plan for training, your Strategic Process Owner (at a minimum), and priority champions.
- A monitoring protocol to keep an eye on progress with priorities and goals.
- An outline for managing monthly, quarterly, and annual meetings and activities.
- A completed Strategic Process Checklist Tool.

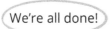 We're all done!　*Woooohooo!!!*

STRATEGY IN MOTION
STRATEGIC MANGEMENT

STRATEGIC PROCESS CHECKLIST

Organization: _____   Date: _____

Strategic Planning Process Checklist

Activity	Activity Owner	Update Frequency	Completion Date	Document Location	Leader Manual	Emp. Manual	Board Manual
Listen and Learn							
Customer Analysis (Top 10 by Revenue, Profit)							
Competitor Analysis (who, offerings, markets)							
Market Analysis (needs, market, share)							
Industry Analysis (5 forces – PEST, trends/challenges)							
Customer Survey (why do they buy from you)							
Employee Survey (Start, Stop, Continue)							
Past Financial statements							
Business Segmentation							
Organization Structure							
Plan Development							
Vision Framework (Purpose, Values, Vision)							
Stakeholder Objectives/Goals							
SWOT – Prioritized							
Target Markets							
Brand Promise / Differentiators							
Product/Service and Market investment strategies (Build, Hold, Divest)							
3-5 Goals and Objectives							
Strategic Priorities, outcomes, and team							

STRETCH
STRATEGIC LEADERS

+1 513.807.6647 | DARCY@STRETCH-SL.COM | STRETCH-SL.COM

FIGURE 9-6
STRATEGIC PROCESS CHECKLIST TOOL
To download, visit stretch-sl.com/SIMtools or follow the QR code in the Preface

Chapter Summary

In this chapter, you:
- Understood the criticality of having the right people to manage and oversee your strategic execution.
- Created a training plan and team charter for leaders of the strategy.
- Considered how to manage strategic priorities and keep the execution in lockstep with the strategic plan.
- Reviewed a meeting schedule and cadence for all the leadership teams.
- Examined the reporting tools that the strategic and priority teams use to track progress.
- Ensured that your strategic plan was complete, but not waiting for perfection!

NOTES

CHAPTER 10

Why Strategies Fail
(And What to Do About It)

"The best strategy is a balance between having a deliberate one, and a flexible, or emergent strategy."

—Clayton Christensen

Why Do Strategies Fail?

I have spent nearly 20 years facilitating strategic plans and have taken more than 400 companies through my process, customized for each one. Once the plan is finished, I have continued to work with a good percentage of them to achieve solid, strategic implementation and communication plans. If the team is stable, you can move forward on strategy; a perfect strategy is never implemented — none of them are ever perfect! All experts agree that the competitive advantage is to be great at execution.

I regularly remind my clients: **"Structure follows strategy,"** so you may need to work through a few people-issues first! This is where your outsourced resources are beneficial. Additionally, I have learned my lesson: if there is distrust in the leadership team, the strategy will fail!

For the past few years, I have partnered with organizational development experts to integrate the "people stuff" with the strategy. I have mentioned Cyndi Wineinger several times and the **critical role organizational development plays in supporting the strategic direction**. This has helped more of my clients be successful and turned ordinary businesses into market leaders — allowing owners to build a great culture, create businesses that are sustaining great customer value, reach stakeholders' objectives, and eventually sell their companies for more than they ever imagined.

In This Chapter

Planning is the easy part; implementation is the real work. There are three main blind spots I will share in this chapter:
- **Your Infrastructure and Your People Need Investment**. Peo-

ple need to know they are an "asset," not a "liability." There are a couple of critical hires to consider. One I prioritize above the rest is a Talent Manager or CPO (Chief People Officer).

- **Marketing and Sales are Not the Same**. The job of marketing is to understand the market, where your products/services will be most successful, then create leads and enable the sales team to close. The job of sales is to close the leads and to manage the relationships to increase share of the account.
- **Communicate, Communicate, Communicate**. Developing the plan is science, communication plans are an art. You will, most likely, need some help with a successful communication and roll-out.

Five Universal Truths

I have found five universal truths working with small- to mid-size companies on the strategic planning journey. These theories were solidified during my 15th year Harvard Business School reunion, listening to Professor Robert Simons. His book, *Seven Strategy Questions: A Simple Approach for Better Execution* reinforced my thinking.[1]

Why? Because it's *your* company!

1. **You Know More About Your Company than I Do**. Or any consultant — this is reality. Even industry experts know less about your company. You are the expert; you have the experience and knowledge. The flip side is also true; I (along with other consultants) know more about our expertise (mine is strategic planning) than you do. **This creates partnership between a company and a consultant**; the consultant helps facilitate process improvement for you. It takes your team's knowledge and experience to help customize the process, which leads to trusted and successful engagement. The universal percentage of companies that fail in strategic implementation is 67%. I believe one reason for this is a cookie-cutter plan that is not owned and developed by the organization. This takes work and the outcome is worth it.

Think of this person as your expert guide!

2. **Strategic Planning Takes Engagement**. You've heard the word engagement a lot lately. Research has shown the higher the engagement, the better the productivity and innovation. Information is retained and understood when people are part of the process. This means your strategic planning team should roll up its sleeves and get to work. I highly recommend each strategic planning team member research a key competitor and interview one or two key customers. Go slowly to go fast and make sure there is plenty of personal engagement in the strategic process.

1 Simons, Robert. *Seven Strategy Questions: A Simple Approach for Better Execution*. Harvard Business Review Press, 2010.

3. **Strategy Does Not Mean a "Right" Answer**. It is a commitment to a process and building strategic capacity to determine the right answers for your company. Based on research done on small businesses, there is a 10-15% industry standard success rate for executing strategic priorities. Remember, it is not a set of events, and every decision gets better with involvement and data. In my experience, this means discussions with managers, team leaders, and team members; it takes open-minded leaders who allocate more time for conversations. Take the time to listen and learn from those who will implement, and your success rate will increase. The implementation success rate of my clients is two to three times the industry standard.

4. **Culture Eats Strategy for Lunch**. When I first started facilitating strategic planning, I would argue with the organizational development consultants over this. I was adamant strategy was the most important process to outperform your peers; the reality is that lots of companies get stuck in implementation. I realized healthy leadership and high-performing teams are critical for a healthy culture and successful strategy. Nowadays, most of my engagements involve an organizational development expert. Cyndi Wineinger and I have created an integrated process that builds healthy leadership teams that are passionate about their culture, while developing a successful strategic planning process. .

It helps to have outside pressure.

5. **The Main Responsibility of the Executive Team is Resource Management**. I highly recommend my clients read, *How Will You Measure Your Life* by Clay Christenson. I had Clay as my Section Leader at Harvard and he constantly reminded us to invest our time and resources in those activities that we prioritize. For example, if we say our health is important, but we don't spend time exercising, is our health really a priority? My point is managing and allocating resources is a critical to support three main activities: (1) Running a healthy business day-to-day (left side of chart below); (2) Managing a strategy and investing in longer-term projects (top of chart); and (3) Being open to "emergent" opportunities and crises (the bottom). **You need to balance all three, which means adjusting and staying flexible.** Take a look at Figure 10-1 on page 174.

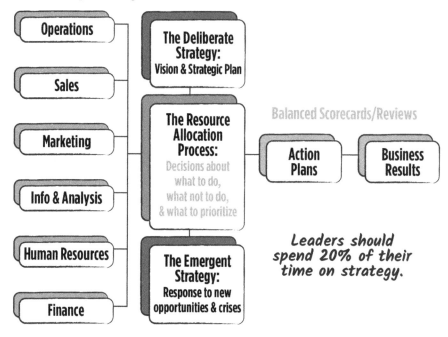

Business results are determined by your alignment & allocation of resources.

FIGURE 10-1
THE RESOURCE ALLOCATION PROCESS

Your Infrastructure and Your People and Need Investment

Working with growth-focused companies, we see a recurring theme: they achieve significant growth then stall because their infrastructure can't keep up. Their revenue doesn't match the structure and processes to sustain. We have seen $100 million organizations constrained by a $30 million infrastructure. Think about your child wearing your suit — it doesn't quite fit yet. They need time to fill-out the suit. **We call this "stretching!"**

Everyone Benefits from Stretching

Most organizations need to play catch-up after significant revenue growth, or better yet, to prepare for growth. This typically means:
- Infrastructure investment.
- Critical strategic hires that need expertise (talent management and marketing are two we see a lot).
- Building capacity for strategy.

These are critical so you don't break good people, especially now! In a fast-growth environment, we are often too busy covering to stop and invest. While this may work for a while, it is NOT sustainable. Soon you will see cracks in the foundation: missed customer expectations, employee burnout, and frustrating process workarounds that take too long.

Years ago, Peter Feil, one of my long-term clients, provided three "easy to understand" categories for people: Leaders, Followers, or Draggers. Of course, you have your "stars," but you might have underperformers or even culture-wreckers at the other end of the spectrum. In the middle, you may have competent folks who are stuck and not able to lock into the vision and future direction of the company.

Good news! If you have gotten this far, you have determined the strategic direction — which was not simple — and you have engaged the extended leadership team to support it. **Now it's time to enlist the rest of the organization to bring it life.**

I can't tell you the number of times I have begged my clients to hire a true talent manager. For some companies, the "people" function is reporting up through the controller or CFO. Let's face it, most of the time, your financial person is more concerned with compliance and liabilities on the P&L and, potentially, less focused on training and development. Managing the "people" systems is a skill set, and if you have a staff of around 75-100 employees, you should consider a full-time "people" person. If you are below that number, you may need to outsource this or find a part-time resource.

Seeking the Missing Person

For a company to move through the growth curves, the way it operates will change. There are critical investments to allocate resources toward key areas of your business to deliver consistent and sustainable growth. These include things like:

- A hiring system and formal onboarding program, both utilizing your new core values and purpose to help people understand your culture immediately.
- Training and development programs for all employees, not just managers. Many of my clients implement IDPs (i.e. Individual Development Plans). This develops key capacity so your managers can successfully delegate and have more time to support the strategic initiatives.
- Understanding data and building dashboards, not just collecting. Data-Analytics is its own skill set.

- Marketing, social media, and your digital presence play in both customer leads and employee recruitment. A hefty 75% of potential employees visit your website to decide if they want to apply. Many check out your social media too.

Marketing and Sales are Not the Same

I'm going to illustrate my hypothesis with a pricing discussion and a customer case study in the following sections. You'll see how easy it can be for good companies to be challenged by who's missing. In my experience, most of my clients have salespeople, unfortunately not many have invested in true marketing resources.

The Pricing Question

I can quickly tell if a company has clear thinking around pricing. When I ask, "How do you approach your pricing strategy?" there are two answers I most commonly hear:

1. ***We add a margin to our cost.*** This means we don't know what our customers are willing to pay, but we know our costs and want to make money. So, we add a margin we *think* is good, and then we *hope* our price is okay. This is the "crossed fingers" strategy I mentioned in the Preface of this book.

2. ***We understand our customers and their Willingness to Pay (WTP).*** *And we know the market and what the competitors are charging, so we price it to be the best choice for our target customers.* This helps capture the total value over our costs. The key is to still be below their WTP.

These two choices are illustrated by the simple diagram in Figure 10-2. You can charge a price based on "cost-plus," but may be leaving money on the table, or worse, it's overpriced. If you understand and effectively communicate your value (preferably something unique), you can charge what the customer is willing to pay.

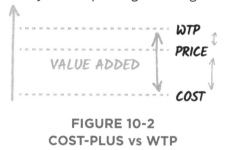

FIGURE 10-2
COST-PLUS vs WTP

What's the difference between the companies that give these widely divergent answers? It's whether or not they have marketing expertise.

- In the "cost-plus" instance, they don't have a marketing person. It is more likely the controller (who understands costs and margins) and the sales manager (who wants the commission) who sets the pricing. It's better than not knowing your costs but is typically set lower than the WTP level you could have asked for.

- In the WTP instance, yes, they understand marketing, have surveyed their customers, and researched the competitive landscape.
- I don't even want to mention the only other pricing mindset. Remember the "hope" strategy; it involves *not* understanding your cost and *not* knowing much about the market. I'm not going to go there.

Marketing helps capture all the value between our cost and the customer's WTP. On the flip side, I have seen companies price things too high, which leads to no revenue, so not a sound, long-term strategy. Compare the scenarios in the graph in Figure 10-3.

In Scenario 1, the cost-plus selling price is higher than the customer's willingness to pay.

No units are sold.

In Scenario 2, the cost-plus selling price is lower than the customer's willingness to pay.

Money is left on the table.

FIGURE 10-3
SCENARIOS FOR WTP

Marketing Should be at the Table

Most small companies have grown with a capable owner and strong sales team. In today's digital world, we have an incredible amount of information and tools for marketing communications (MARCOM) well. Indeed, your competitive advantage comes from marketing doing what it's there for — understanding the market and communicating the *unique value* you bring to customers. **Another way to think**

of marketing is sales-enablement. Marketing helps generate the leads and sales closes them. Of course, you need a strong sales focus as well.

In this case study, I cast the net a bit wider and look at an exceptional company, whose general manager struggled with really understanding the role of marketing.

CASE STUDY

Gearbox Manufacturer and Distributor

One of my longest and dearest clients is the "Gold Standard" for gearboxes — a built-to-order distributor for demanding environments.

Over the years, I have learned a great deal from their general manager and entire leadership team. The company invested in a very capable leadership team and successfully grew the company each year. I loved his organizational chart because it was upside down; he and his leadership team were at the bottom.

With a savvy sales team and big opportunities in the 24/7 food market, they excelled at selling through manufacturer reps and growing this segment. The highly skilled sales teams pulled their product through the market. Since they had such a strong brand and value proposition in this segment, the GM would often comment, **"I have no idea what marketing does."** At this point, the sales team did most of their own marketing.

I would ask, "How did they get such a strong brand in this market?" We would discuss this a bit about this and then move on. At this point, they had a very strong position in this market. I knew someday soon it would reach a tipping point.

Fast forward 10 years: the market was changing with new competitors and better products. On top of that, their stakeholder goals revealed a revenue gap over the next five years; it was time to find and grow new markets. They needed research, new customers, and the tools to develop new sales. They had tipped and now needed marketing expertise to support.

"This is marketing," I reminded the GM. Marketing's main job is to create and generate leads finding opportunities for sales to push into these target markets and ideal customers. Sales close the leads. This was a significant change for the organization. They needed a radically different go-to-market

---

strategy, moving from being "pulled" in the food market to "pushing" themselves into new markets.

At about the same time, the sales channels were exploding, and an online presence was required, but there was hesitation — they were unsure if this was a good idea. It was time to admit it's not all about sales. It was time to invest in a new structure, people, and skills. It was a challenging time for the organization and required a lot of "pushing." Over the next year, they invested in marketing, redefined their sales structure, added inside sales/customer service, and began to develop the processes and tools they needed to grow into new markets.

What Does Marketing Do? *Great question!*

We think we understand marketing, but it is a misunderstood expertise and often an underutilized area for small businesses. Many of my clients believe marketing is about building a website, running ads, writing blogs, sending mass emails, managing social media — in other words, "tactics." It's typically the last role to get hired and the first to get fired when the going gets tough.

Most companies, even today, do little marketing and rely on the "pull" strategy, meaning they pick up the phone when a customer calls. **I refer to this as the "answer the phone" strategy**. This works well if the right customers are calling and are willing to pay the right price.

Another common statement I hear is, "Our product (or service) is different," to which I respond, "In what way? How would anyone know, and does anyone care?" It is amazing how many companies think their product is different but do little to communicate *what* is different to their customers.

Strategy is about determining what it means to win — finding what is unique and different about your company, and even more importantly, communicating it. **Marketing's job is to research and understand who your customers are and what they really want.** Surprisingly, many companies have never completed a customer survey and have little more than a formal connection with their customers. If your sales team is the sole voice of the customer, they believe *price* is the reason customers buy. In survey after survey after survey, price is commonly the *third* reason customers buy — it is your job to identify the top two. Even more importantly, based on those top two, what are your customers really willing to pay? And how do we market to them better based on their top two reasons *and* price?

Marketing needs to be at the table when strategic planning is underway. Strategic planning helps identify target markets and the products and services mix that brings the most value to those target markets. Marketing should be charged with research to contribute to that analysis and help define value from the customer's point of view. Figure 10-4 is one of those concepts that's an "oldie but goodie" — it defines the range where marketing is the biggest contributor and can make a game-changing difference.[2]

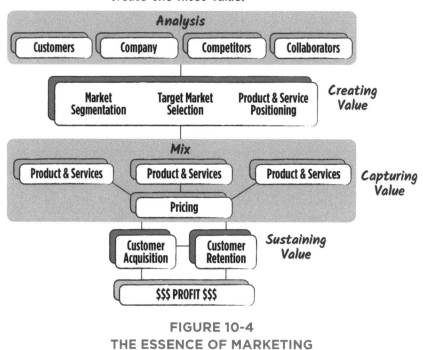

Define the target markets where you create the most value.

FIGURE 10-4
THE ESSENCE OF MARKETING

Brand Promise

During strategic planning, you may have noticed a reference to "brand promise" on the Strategic Plan Summary Tool. Asking, "What is our brand promise?" is a key strategic question, and when I ask about this, I often get blank stares. It's a marketing term that captures the essence of your value.

The brand promise is based on your key differentiators for your core product/services in your key market (this does not mean every-

2   Dolan, Robert. *Notes on Marketing Strategy*. Harvard Business Review, 1997.

thing to everybody). This information can come from your customer interviews (**Listen and Learn**) and from research that marketing can do in the broader market — especially when you're trying to explore new markets, products, or services.

Remember, many customers believe it is their job to get the "best" price possible; it's your responsibility to communicate why your product or service is better and why they should pay more. Yep, back to another value of marketing! When marketing and sales work together the goal is to deeply understand "why" your customers buy from you and develop the plan to best communicate. In other words, how you are competing, and winning, in the market.

How You Compete

As you expand beyond your current markets or products/services, you want to put distance between the reasons for the buying decisions and price considerations. The more the customer chooses your products/services for important value considerations, the fewer competitors you have. If no other company has what you have, and someone (a customer) wants it, guess who sets the price? You do!

FIGURE 10-5
PRODUCT/SERVICE COMPETITION: INCREASING WTP

How does this work?
1. It starts with a need coming from the market (thanks, marketing!) with a new **function** (something a customer wants/needs). You may have this market niche to yourself for a while, so you need to act fast — just make sure you know what your return might be for investing in developing the function.
2. The next thing the customer will pay for is better **reliability/quality**. Consumers will pay more for a product/service with

higher quality, that lasts longer, or has better reliability. Data should be mostly used in these claims. For example, the gearboxes in the case study above had data to prove their equipment lasted longer, so their customers were willing to pay a premium for the higher quality.

3. The final dimension is that customers may pay more for **convenience**; how you package it, where they purchase it, and customer service. Service is a big opportunity to smaller companies if they spend the time to be different. For example, if I need a box of Fruit Loops, but I don't want to go to the grocery store. Instead, I go to the "convenience" store. Guess what? I will pay more for it! Most of the time, a lot more!

Convenience isn't just about convenience store products — it applies to almost everything we buy. From groceries to cars to online delivery of services, buyers want to choose carefully but then buy with velocity. Increasingly, shoppers don't want to interact with you. You need marketing to manage the interaction in a way that gives the buyer what they want when they want it.

Let's say you see a market need (thanks again, marketing!) to develop a **new function** that customers want/need. The moment you have a competitor offering the same function, the price becomes an issue. Companies that invest in research and development strategically price their product to achieve a return on their investment *before* competitors enter the market. Unfortunately, many new products fail due to lack of research, and, in turn, customers aren't willing to pay the premium for the new function because they don't value it.

Back to function, reliability, and convenience. If the market sees all these things as the same (or doesn't care about the differences), they will pick the **cheapest option** — that's the definition of the commodity market and not easy for a small business to win.

CASE STUDY

Hospital-Grade TV Manufacturer

A good example is a company I worked with that made TVs specifically for the hospital market. In the beginning, they carved a "niche" with their customized product. Very few competitors offered hospital-grade TVs, and their margins were great. As more competitors saw the same opportunity, my client focused on higher quality and better reliability (longer lasting).

Unfortunately, large competitors came into the market and convinced some hospitals it was just a TV, and they shouldn't care about it being "hospital-grade" TV. As a result, these hospitals chose the least expensive option.

Communicate, Communicate, Communicate

Internal communication is a critical part of the strategic roll-out and engagement process. Get support from your marketing team (or hire a marketing agency) to develop your strategic communication plan. Develop a broad and deep plan, so all employees understand their role to deliver the strategic plan.

Here are some best practices to consider:

- **Utilize graphs and pictures** to communicate key strategic concepts (i.e., your core values). Remember 65% more information is retained in a picture versus text.
- **Create a strategic infographic** focused on the key parts of the strategy: purpose, values, vision, core focus, brand promise, and strategic priorities.
- **Utilize your company newsletter**, internet, or weekly/monthly email with strategic reminders and strategic update.
- **Add your strategic direction to your hiring, onboarding, and training systems**. Many companies are describing their culture in job postings or videos to make sure they attract people who will fit with the culture they desire.
- **Reinforce key strategic concepts on your website, social media, and in customer communications**. I have my core values at the bottom of my emails. Make sure your "About Us" page spells out your purpose and core values. Most of the time, vision statements are internal and meant to inspire the organization.

Picture excellence across all your key people, each driving their teams toward the strategic goals you set yourself. Marketing helps them message internally to keep everyone inspired, focused, and engaged; it's all about engagement.

Final Thoughts

Great people build great cultures, so it's likely that *your* vision for the company's culture will align with the employees' vision. You took the time to develop the plan, now invest the time to bring in the right people and communicate, support, and live it!

I will leave you with the note my daughter's tennis coach, Adam Moler. Coach Adam, the Saint Ursula tennis team, delivered this at the beginning of one of their matches her sophomore year. Lily was so inspired by this, she asked if she could have it. Years later it is still on our refrigerator. I share this often with my clients!

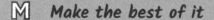

M Make the best of it

I Inspire others

N Never give up

D Do whatever you can

S Something worth doing deserves full effort

E Each day is a new opportunity

T Try first, try again, try more

—Coach Adam, 2019

NOTES

NOTES

Darcy Bien

Darcy Bien is a strategist who has helped hundreds of companies achieve their vision. With more than 20 years of experience, her national reputation is built upon delivering actionable strategy. The daughter of a brilliant entrepreneur who struggled with execution may explain Darcy's

bulldog tenacity for doing whatever it takes to achieve successful strategic implementation.

Her debut book, *Strategy in Motion: A Proven Playbook for Companies Who Win*, outlines the anatomy of strategic planning and the best tools to drive results. Jam-packed with memorable anecdotes that show her ideas in practice, the book is a must-have guide for companies who are new to planning and for those who have plans collecting dust on the shelf.

Darcy was a partner of a strategy focused firm, Partners in Change, since 2001. Recently, she is co-founder of Stretch Strategic Leaders, a consultancy for strategic planning and leadership development. She holds an MBA from Harvard Business School and a BS in Mechanical Engineering from Georgia Institute of Technology.

Darcy resides in Cincinnati, Ohio, with her husband, their three ambitious children, and two dogs who love to run with her!

APPENDIX 1

The *Strategy In Motion™ Process*

Strategy in Motion™ is a four-phase process for developing and successfully executing a strategy for your company.

STRATEGY *IN MOTION*™

1 LISTEN AND LEARN
» Complete strategic assessment
» Understand stakeholder goals
» Listen to employees and customers
» Analyze external environment

2 PLAN DEVELOPMENT
» Agree on current reality
» Define desired state
» Determine strategic choices
» Outline strategic priorities

3 IMPLEMENTATION
» Create scorecards and plans
» Update structure
» Link to teams
» Communicate to organization

4 STRATEGIC MANAGEMENT
» "Look up" monthly
» Assess quarterly
» Update annually
» Invest in training

Phases 1 and 2 cover the development of a strategic plan, and Phases 3 and 4 cover how to implement and create strategic management around the implementation. Each phase comes with tools illustrated and described in the relevant chapters. A list of tools is provided on page 190.

The tools listed below are downloadable from **stretch-sl.com/SIMtools** or by following the QR code in the Preface:

Phase 1: Listen and Learn
Strategic Planning Assessment Tool
Strategic Planning Team Tool
Stakeholder Goals Tool
Current Momentum Tool
Pre-Plan Tool: Business Segmentation
Strategic Survey Tool
Board/Advisor Survey Tool
Key Customer Interview Tool
Competitive Analysis Tool
7 Factor External Analysis Tool

Phase 2: Plan Development
SWOT: External/Internal Analysis Tool
Strategic Plan Summary: Current Reality Tool
Strategic Plan Key Concepts Tool
Plan Development: Strategic Priority Tool
Strategic Plan Summary: Strategic Choices Tool
Business Segmentation Forecast Tool
Strategic Plan Summary: Desired State Tool

Phase 3: Implementation
Implementation Checklist Tool
Strategy Scorecard Tool
Run-the-Business Balanced Scorecard Tool
Priority Action Plan Tool
Team Meeting Calendar Tool
6 Core Strategic Questions Tool

Phase 4: Strategic Management
Internal Strategic Planner: Certification Checklist
Quarterly Priority Review Tool
Strategic Process Checklist Tool

APPENDIX 2
The Stretch Strategic Bootcamp Program

Nearly 400 companies have used Darcy Bien's **Strategy in Motion™ Process** to deliver 2.2 times the industry's standard implementation rate.

Learn from her 20+ years of experience in customizing strategic planning best practices for growth-oriented, mid-size companies.

Kickstart Your Strategic Planning with Our Flexible, Online Bootcamp Program!

Acquire the skills you need to strategically grow your business, team, or department in the new reality. With four self-paced modules, this Bootcamp will equip you with the necessary process and resources to create a winning strategy. Many key assumptions have changed, and it is critical to understand why, what, and how to move forward.

FOR EXECUTIVES, LEADERS, AND DEPARTMENT MANAGERS WHO WANT TO WIN AT STRATEGY.

WHAT YOU WILL LEARN:

- The framework and building blocks of creating a strategy to be successful
- The integral role of PEOPLE and STRATEGY needed to propel your business/team forward
- Key strategic concepts everyone in your organization should know
- Critical tools to customize for your organization

HOW YOU WILL BENEFIT:

- Acquire the skills you need to win at strategy
- Learn best practices, vignettes, and articles to expand your strategic knowledge
- Leave with a strategic toolkit of 25+ best practices customized for mid-size companies

CERTIFICATION (optional) Designed for Process Owners:

As part of your **Bootcamp**, receive the **Strategy in Motion**™ Certification Guide and work through the tools and process at your pace. It also includes phone support and in-person (or virtual, if needed) certification. The four steps to certification are:

1. Complete the Certification Checklist
2. Take the online Bootcamp
3. Develop your strategy
4. Complete your certification

FOR MORE INFORMATION:

- **513.807.6647 | info@stretch-sl.com | stretch-sl.com**
- More details and enrollment: **https://stretch-bootcamp-training. teachable.com/p/stretch-strategic-bootcamp**
  - Discount code: **STRETCH**

Client Strategic Infographic Examples

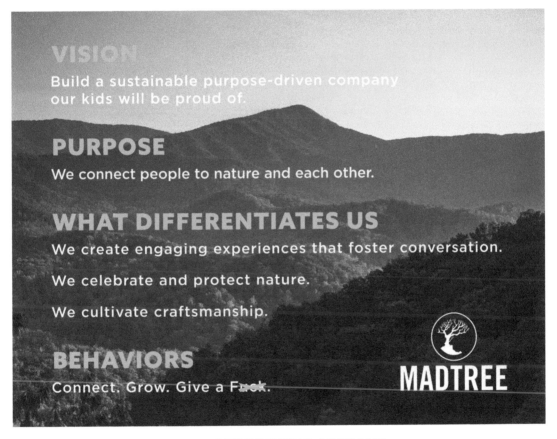

MADTREE BREWING COMPANY

PURPOSE
Deliver peace of mind in the demanding world of motion

VISION
The gold standard for perfect motion

MISSION
STOBER puts things in motion...
...integrally and precisely
...as a team and with personality
...responsibly and in a forward-looking manner

WE ARE STOBER.
CONNECTED. COMMITTED. COMPASSIONATE.

THE BIG PICTURE
We think in terms of integrated solutions

TEAMWORK
We embrace teamwork

QUALITY
Quality is in our DNA

INNOVATION
Innovation is what drives us

DEDICATION
We give our all for mutual success

RESPONSIBILITY
Sustainable growth is our top priority

MISSION STATEMENT

STOBER DRIVES INC

PURPOSE

To transform the hospitality industry by improving lives through our culture of caring.

VISION

To elicit genuine JOY from each and every guest, community, and employee we serve.

MISSION

To celebrate life through impeccable experiences and impactful emotional connections.

SERVANT'S HEART
Icon: The Heart

The heart symbolizes caring, compassion, kindness and hospitality. The outward moving lines symbolize light in the darkness, helping others find their way.

CHANGE THE GAME
Icon: The Knight

The knight literally changes the game of chess. The knight is the only piece that can "jump over" other pieces, it moves in ways that other pieces can't in order to achieve its goals.

HUSTLE
Icon: The Flame

The flame represents the internal fire and irresistable force that drives us to outperform the competition and propels us to success, no matter what the odds are.

BE EXCEPTIONAL
Icon: The Star

An industry-wide symbol of excellence, and achievement, the star reminds us what we're here to do everyday - be the best, do what's right, and outshine everyone.

TRUE-TO-SELF
Icon: The Dove

The dove is a universal symbol of purity and truth, reinforcing our value of being true-to-self. The dove has the ability to rise above; it is a standard bearer for distinction and unwavering authenticity.

JEFF RUBY CULINARY ENTERTAINMENT

PARALLAX ADVANCED RESEARCH

List of Figures

Figures with "C" at the end are Client Examples.

CPSIA information can be obtained
at www.ICGtesting.com
Printed in the USA
LVHW070725141122
733067LV00003B/24